Carlo Gébler as born in Dublin, 1954. He is a graduate of the University of York in English Literature, and of the National Film and Television School. His first novel, *The Eleventh Summer* was published in 1985. More recently he published *The Cure* (1994) and *How to Murder a Man* (1998) as well as the short story collection *W. 9 & Other Lives.Dance of Death* is his first venture into drama. He currently writer-in-residence, H.M.P. Maghaberry, Co. Antrim. He is married with five children. He lives outside Enniskillen in Co. Fermanagh.

By the same author

Fiction
The Eleventh Summer
August in July
Work & Play
Malachy and his Family
Life of a Drum
The Cure
How to Murder a Man
W9 & Other Lives

Non-fiction
Driving Through Cuba: An East-West Journey
The Glass Curtain: Inside an Ulster Community

Children's fiction
The T.V. Genie
The Witch that Wasn't
The Base
Frozen Out

DANCE OF DEATH

DANCE OF DEATH

A version of August Strindberg's Dance of Death

CARLO GÉBLER

LAGAN PRESS
BELFAST
2000

The author wishes to acknowledge the financial support of *An Chomhairle Ealaíon*/The Arts Council. All inquiries regarding amateur and professional performance of these works should be addressed to Antony Harwood, c/o Gillon Aitken and Associates, 29 Fernshaw Road, London, SW10 0TG.

Published by
Lagan Press
7 Lower Crescent, Belfast, BT7 1NR

ISBN: 1 873687 58 3
Author: Gébler, Carlo
Title: Dance of Death
2000

Cover Design: December Publications
Set in New Baskerville
Printed by Noel Murphy Printing, Belfast

for Nicolas Kent, who made it happen

CONTENTS

Author's Note	11
Dance of Death, Part One	*17*
Dance of Death, Part Two	*69*
Letters to Nicolas Kent	*117*

Author's Note

Aged sixteen, I picked up Strindberg's *Occult Diary*. At first it was like being stuck in a lift with a lunatic; but then, after a few pages, irritation gave way to appalled fascination, which in turn gave way to admiration. Yes, it was mad but so vivid, so psychologically true.

Next I read *Inferno*. The book didn't describe Strindberg's madness, it was his madness and to read it was to *know* Strindberg's state of mind. The book literally changed me—I was different when I finished from what I had been when I started—and only a very few writers can do this to a reader.

After the prose it was on to the plays (brilliant) and then the films of Ingmar Bergman, Strindberg's leading living advocate.

I wish it had been my idea to re-translate *Dance of Death* but it was Nick Kent's. He made the suggestion by phone early in January 1997. I immediately wanted in and re-read the plays. *Part One* was great, a play that went like a Swiss watch. *Part Two*, on the other hand was febrile, melodramatic. If this was a watch, then it was running far too fast.

So what to do? First a new setting was determined. The plays would be set, immediately before partition, on an imaginary British Army garrison island off the north-west coast of Ireland. I then set about translating and Hibernising *Part One*. My text is Strindberg's although I have made it more pointed in places.

Part Two was a different proposition. First I made a detailed breakdown of the narrative elements as Strindberg had written them. Then I cut everything that didn't work or wouldn't fit the Irish setting.

Then I took what I had left (and there was some left—all of it brilliant) and filled the spaces in-between. It was unlike anything I'd ever written before because so much was already laid down.

The development of the characters in *Part Two* had to follow on from what had happened in *Part One* and the story had to be the same story Strindberg told (even if I told it in a different way). It was like writing a crossword crossed with restoring an old master.

I also decided (at Nick Kent's suggestion) to set the second part at the time of the Irish Rising, Easter 1916 (which was not in Strindberg's original of course). The theme of *Dance of Death* is betrayal and it seemed that since my version was located in a British military garrison in the early twentieth century, then *the* event which epitomized betrayal from the point of view of the British Army in Ireland was surely the right one to have as a backdrop.

***

August Strindberg (1849-1912) wrote *Part One* of *Dance of Death* in October 1900, at exactly the same time as he wrote *Easter*. Two more different plays it would be hard to imagine, the first dark, the second uplifting, even hopeful, but then Strindberg had an amazing capacity to contain within his mind contradictory ideas and moods.

For the immediate history of the play, we need to go back to 1899. Strindberg had returned to Stockholm from abroad and he began to see a great deal of his sister, Anna (1855-1937), and her husband, Hugo Philp (1844-1906), a schoolmaster .

Relations between the playwright, his sister and her husband were freighted with a great deal of history, some good, some bad. During a row in 1876, about family money and who should inherit, Hugo Philp had taken August's side. As a result, Strindberg's father had excommunicated both August and Anna.

In 1884, ten years later, when Strindberg had been vilified for his short stories, *Getting Married*, Philp had supported him. But then, ten years later again, the playwright turned on his friend (such fallings out were typical in Strindberg's feud-filled life). Strindberg then included a repellent description of Hugo in *Vivisections*.

This should have signalled the end of relations but Anna and Hugo were rather kinder and more forgiving than the irascible

August. In 1896, when the playwright was in Paris, penniless, alone and nearly mad, Philps visited and comforted him. *Vivisections* was forgotten, relations were restored, and in the summer of 1899, Hugo and Anna Philp invited the author to stay at their house in the Stockholm archipelago

To begin, everything was marvellous (good beginnings leading on to awful middles and worse ends were a trait of Strindberg's life). As reported by Märta Philp, Hugo and Anna's daughter, the playwright enjoyed sitting in the evening sun, drinking wine and listening to Anna playing the piano. Anna had trained as a violinist and had won a scholarship to study in Paris in her late teens. She didn't take this up but married Hugo instead.

In January, 1900, Hugo became ill with diabetes. Strindberg took to visiting the patient, sitting up all night with him, and talking about God, death and the universe. In June, the Philps moved from Stockholm to Furusund, and August went with them. Once again Anna entertained her guest on the piano and the adults played cards. But then Hugo had the temerity to defend some writers Strindberg loathed; he also criticised August for the way the writer had treated his first wife, Siri. An argument followed, inevitably; Strindberg hated criticism but jealousy was also involved. He was strongly attracted to his sister, sexually, physically, emotionally, and so his row with Hugo was fuelled by the antagonism a suitor feels towards a rival. The fall out was terrible and before June was out, Strindberg retired to Stockholm, smouldering with rage.

Having quarreled with Hugo, Strindberg now developed a violent hatred for his brother-in-law as well as his sister. On October 5th, the Philps celebrated their silver wedding anniversary but Strindberg did not attend, not that he seemed to mind. Conflict, far from harming or upsetting Strindberg, had quite the reverse effect. It filled him with energy, it was the well-spring of his art.

Strindberg began work on the *Dance of Death* on October 9th, 1900 and was finished by October 31st, 1900. As always, he worked at tremendous speed. However, the play was not simply dashed out. Strindberg had made lengthy notes regarding characters before he put pen to paper. These documentary materials also show that he wrote with no thought of a sequel. The title he took from the French composer Charles Camille Saint-Saëns, whose composition *La Danse Macabre*, he had, at one stage, intended to include in the play.

Strindberg was also much influenced in composition by the Swedish natural scientist and religious thinker, Emanuel Swedenborg (1688-1772), to whose works he turned after his breakdown in Paris. He was particularly attracted to Swedenborg's assertions regarding "marriages of Hell". According to Swedenborg, partners in such marriages, although often greatly excited sexually by each other, also burned with a murderous hatred; this was a hatred so enormous, it was not possible to describe it in words.

However, the play was not only the product of reading; it was also very much the product of Strindberg's recent life experience, most notably his up and down relationship with the Philps, on whom Edgar and Alice, the couple in the play, are modelled. Alice, for example, is an actress of some standing who has given up her career to marry Edgar, just as Anna aborted her musical training in order to marry Hugo. Edgar, like Hugo, suddenly falls seriously ill. But perhaps the most telling similarity is the way Strindberg's proxy in the play—called Kurt in the original, Conor in my version—covets Edgar's wife even as he sits at the bedside of the man he secretly yearns to replace, just as Strindberg courted his sister, Anna, as he sat at the bedside of his brother-in-law, Hugo Philp. Other echoes of real life must include the silver wedding anniversary which Edgar and Alice are about to celebrate, surely a reference to the anniversary Strindberg did not attend in 1900, and the endless card games. Hugo was certainly in no doubt that the character of Edgar was modelled on himself, for after reading a copy of the play through for the first time, it is reported that he promptly threw the text on the fire.

Strindberg wrote *Part Two* at the end of 1900, probably in December. His German translator, Emil Schering, when preparing his translation of *Part One*, had wondered whether the work wasn't so pessimistic as to make it unlikely that it would ever be staged in Germany. Prompted by this remark, it seems possible that Strindberg wrote the sequel, *Part Two*, with its more hopeful ending (as least as far as the younger generation is concerned). However, from the notes he prepared for *Part One*, it is also clear from the very start that, though he had no thought of a sequel, he had always had in mind the idea that feuding families could be reconciled by their children—as happily happened in his own case *vis-a-vis* the Philps, when in 1907 his daughter, Greta, married Henry Philp, son of Hugo and Anna.

Carlo Gébler
11th February, 1998

Characters in *Dance of Death*

Part One

Captain Edgar Dawson, commanding officer of a coastal artillery
installation
Alice Dawson (née Coyne), his wife, an ex-actress
Conor Coyne, newly appointed Quarantine Master, and Alice's
cousin
Mary, the maid
Eileen, an old woman
Sentry

Part Two
Dawson, Alice, Conor Coyne and Sentry as in Part One.
Judith, Edgar and Alice's daughter
Aidan, Conor's son
Lieutenant Johnston, a junior officer, English

DANCE OF DEATH
Part One

This version of *Dance of Death, Part One,* was first presented at the Tricycle Theatre London, Thursday 19th March, 1998. The play was directed by Nicolas Kent. The designer was Monica Frawley. The cast was:

Captain Edgar Dawson	Michael Cochrane
Alice Dawson	Marion Bailey
Conor Coyne	Tim Woodward
Mary & Eileen	Olivia Caffrey
Sentry	Dean Loxton

Edgar is in a Heavy Regiment of the Royal Artillery. The place is a British military facility on Crookedstone island off the north-west coast of County Donegal. It is early autumn, 1913.

ACT ONE

SCENE 1

The interior of a Martello Tower, a circular fortress built during the Napoleonic period. First a powder magazine, then a prison, now it is a dwelling. The walls are grey stone and forbidding.

At the back of the room there are three doorways—a pair of French doors that open onto a battlement, a door to a porch with a front door that opens onto a yard underneath the battlement, and an internal door that opens onto a corridor that leads to the kitchen and the stairs to the upper storey.

Outside the French doors we can see long range guns lined along the battlement. The ends of the gun barrels have a protective canvas sock fitted over them. (The Great War is still almost a year away). In the distance stretches the sea.

In the room there is an upright piano, a sewing table with armchairs around it, a writing table with a telegraph apparatus on it, a writing desk with flap down top and drawers, a chaise-longue, a sideboard with bottles and glasses, a square stove with a door, a mercury barometer, a ceiling lamp, and a whatnot, framed family photographs on top and a windup gramophone with a horn trumpet underneath.

One part of the room is devoted to Alice's theatrical career—there is an oil painting of Alice in scanty costume with dusty laurel wreaths hanging off the top corners of the frame, several framed Edwardian playbills with the name Alice Coyne prominent at the top, a mortar board, and a scroll in Latin that looks like a university diploma. In another area—the 'military' corner—there is a 'Trafalgar' wardrobe filled with uniforms, and a long line of wall hooks heavy with belts, swords, holsters, scabbards, binoculars, helmets and other kinds of military paraphernalia.

It is unsettling to have so much crammed into so small a space.

A mild evening, October, autumnal. The French doors at the back are thrown open. We can see a SENTRY *with a rifle moving up and down, the barrel glimmering in the glow of the setting sun*

The CAPTAIN *sits in an armchair.* ALICE *sits in another armchair. The* CAPTAIN *fingers a half-smoked cigar. He lights the cigar with a match, inhales, coughs, puts the cigar down.* ALICE *touches the hair piled high on top of her head. She looks as if she is waiting for something unpleasant to happen.*

CAPTAIN: Get off that rump and play me something.

ALICE [*wearily, not rising to the bait*]: Anything in mind?

CAPTAIN: You choose.

ALICE: You never liked my repertoire.

CAPTAIN: You never liked mine! [*After a pause*] Well, that's that.

ALICE: Do you feel a draught?

CAPTAIN: I'll close the doors if you want.

ALICE: No, it's all right. [*Pause*] You've stopped smoking?

CAPTAIN: Strong tobacco doesn't agree with me any more.

ALICE [*almost amiably*]: Upmann's are mild ... you should get some! ... smoking's your only pleasure.

CAPTAIN: Pleasure ... sorry, what's that?

ALICE: I know no more about the subject than you ... ready for your whiskey yet?

CAPTAIN: No. What's the fodder tonight?

ALICE: I don't know. Ask Kitty ... she's the cook.

CAPTAIN: We'll be hitting the mackerel season soon.

ALICE: God! Winter already!

CAPTAIN: Yes ... short bright days, crisp frosty nights, a grilled mackerel, with pepper and lemon, and a glass of Mâcon ... paradise.

ALICE: You should have been on stage, not me!

CAPTAIN: That Mâcon of mine, any left in the cellar?

ALICE: What! We haven't had a cellar for five years.

CAPTAIN: Don't be so ignorant. I shall have to lay in some wine for our Silver Wedding—

ALICE: You are joking?

CAPTAIN: No, I'm not.

ALICE: Ah, why hide our quarter-century of misery when you can share it with the garrison!

CAPTAIN: You exaggerate as always. We've had some sport ... and children. Besides, one must enjoy life because when it's over ... that's it.

ALICE: Really?

CAPTAIN: Once the spark's out, you're a barrowful of garden muck.

ALICE: A whole life to end up ... as fertilizer.

CAPTAIN: Not my fault. It's just the way it is. [*Pause*]

ALICE: Any sign of the post?

CAPTAIN: Yes.

ALICE: And the children's school bill?

CAPTAIN: Yes.

ALICE: It's like drawing teeth. How much *is* the school bill?

CAPTAIN [*takes bill from his pocket, puts on pince-nez, takes his pince-nez off again*]: Eyes have packed up. You read it.

ALICE: Oh dear, something wrong with your eyes?

CAPTAIN: Seemingly.

ALICE: You know what it is?

CAPTAIN: Tell me.

ALICE: Old age.

CAPTAIN: Balderdash. [*Pause*] Me?

ALICE: Yes, you. There's nothing wrong with me.

CAPTAIN: You can't help yourself, can you?

ALICE [*looking at the bill*]: Can you pay this?

CAPTAIN: Yes ... not immediately.

ALICE: Pay it now ... next year you'll be retired, on a small pension the War Office'll always pay late, and you'll be ill—

CAPTAIN: Stop it! I'm never ill, just out of sorts today. And don't worry ... I'll live another twenty years!

ALICE: That's not what Doctor Haverty thinks.

CAPTAIN: Sawbones!

ALICE: As opposed, I suppose, to you, the professional physician!

CAPTAIN: I'm not ill, I never will be ... and I'll die with my boots on, like an old soldier!

[*A brass band starts up faintly in the distance.*]

ALICE: Talking of the Doctor, he's giving a party tonight!

CAPTAIN: So what! Oh! you mean, why weren't we invited? Easy ... because we don't mix and I loathe him and Maureen. Riff-raff.

ALICE: That's what you call everybody.

CAPTAIN: Because everybody is riff-raff.

ALICE: Except you.

CAPTAIN: Whatever life's thrown at me, I've always been a gentleman. That's the difference between them and me.

[*Pause. The sound of the brass band, louder than before.*]

ALICE: Game of whist?

CAPTAIN: Why the hell not!

ALICE [*taking a pack of cards from the drawer of a table and beginning to shuffle*]: He's got the regimental band over from Derry.

CAPTAIN [*angry*]: Doesn't surprise me ... he's always ingratiating himself with the Colonel. Think if I'd chosen—

ALICE [*dealing*]: Maureen was my friend until she cheated me—

CAPTAIN: They're all cheats ... what's trumps?

ALICE: Put on your glasses!

CAPTAIN: They won't help ... come on.

ALICE: Spades.

CAPTAIN [*irritated*]: Spades.

ALICE [*playing a card*]: No one likes us ... not even the lonely wives of the new officers.

CAPTAIN [*playing and taking trick*]: Who cares? We don't give parties, they don't get the chance to tell us they don't like us ... and I'm fine on my own.

ALICE [*playing card*]: I never complained ... but our children grew up here knowing nobody.

CAPTAIN [*playing card*]: They're big now, they can make their own friends. [*Triumphantly*] The last is mine!

ALICE [*taking trick*]: I don't think so.

CAPTAIN: Eight and six makes fifteen.

ALICE: Fourteen.

CAPTAIN: I've forgotten how to count. [*Yawning*] My deal.

ALICE: Go to bed if you're tired.

[*The brass band again.*]

CAPTAIN [*dealing*]: With that racket?

ALICE: Music carries such a long way. Do you think Conor was asked?

CAPTAIN: Well, he arrived this morning ... so he certainly had time to get togged up even if not to come and see us.

ALICE: If he's Quarantine Master, does that mean a quarantine?

CAPTAIN: I don't know.

ALICE: Strange, my cousin, here. We once shared a name—

CAPTAIN: What's that to be proud of?

ALICE: I don't run your family down—I expect the same from you.

CAPTAIN: Here we go!

ALICE: Do you have to be a doctor to be the Quarantine Master?

CAPTAIN: No! The Q.M. is just a glorified ledger clerk cum typist. What's amazing is Conor *is* neither.

ALICE: Leave him alone, poor thing—

CAPTAIN: He chose to dump his wife and child, I didn't, plus he cost me.

ALICE: Never forget a wrong, do you?

CAPTAIN: But it's the truth, isn't it? And remember what happened in America? I haven't missed him, but he was a nice enough lad. Good in an argument.

ALICE: Yes, didn't he always give in to you?

CAPTAIN: You would see it that way ... no, he was a man I could talk to.

ALICE: It's strange, Conor coming now, our silver wedding anniversary—

CAPTAIN: Why strange? Oh, I see ... because he affianced us.

ALICE: Well, he did, didn't he?

CAPTAIN: Yes. Conor was seized by an idea, after which ... but you know the story better than I do.

ALICE: It was really more a notion wasn't it? ... than a plan—

CAPTAIN: And one I've had to pay for ... while he got off scot-free.

ALICE: How different my life would be if I'd stayed in the theatre. All my friends are famous now.

CAPTAIN: Oh no, we're not back on that again, are we? Now I do need a drink. [*The* CAPTAIN *goes to the sideboard; he pours a whiskey, squirts in soda and starts to drink while standing.*] You know what we need? A brass foot rail ... like the Gresham hotel or the Shelbourne.

ALICE: Well, why not have one made to remind us. Those glory days in Dublin were my happiest, you know.

CAPTAIN [*drinks quickly*]: Do you remember the charlotte russe at Monsieur Jammets? [*He smacks his lips.*]

ALICE: No, but I remember the concerts at the Rotunda.

CAPTAIN: You're such a highbrow, aren't you?

ALICE: You should be proud to have a wife as cultivated—

CAPTAIN: I didn't say I wasn't!

ALICE: Without my qualities you'd have nothing to boast about—

CAPTAIN: They're hitting the floor at the Doctor's now ... hear the trombones? ... oomp-pah-pah, oomp-pah-pah—

ALICE: How long since I danced a waltz?

CAPTAIN: You wouldn't still be up to it?

ALICE: Would you?

CAPTAIN: Your dancing days are done. Like mine.

ALICE: I'm ten years younger than you.

CAPTAIN: A lady's always ten years younger than a gentleman.

ALICE: You're over the hill. I'm entering my prime.

CAPTAIN: You don't know how delightful you are ... with other men.

ALICE: May I light the lamp?

CAPTAIN: As you wish.

ALICE: Ring, please!

[*The* CAPTAIN *goes to the desk and rings the handbell.* MARY *enters through the door from the kitchen area.*]

CAPTAIN: Mary, I wonder if you'd be so good—

ALICE: Just tell her to light the lamp.

MARY: Yes, madam.

[*With the* CAPTAIN *watching,* MARY *lights the ceiling lamp.*]

ALICE: Did you trim the wick?

MARY: Of course.

ALICE: How dare you talk—

CAPTAIN: Stop it—

ALICE [*to* MARY]: Go on. I'll deal with the lamp myself.

MARY: Yes, you'd better.

ALICE [*rising from armchair*]: Get out.

MARY: What would you do if I really did leave?

[MARY *goes. The* CAPTAIN *lowers the lamp wick.*]

ALICE [*anxiously*]: Do you think she'll ... actually go?

CAPTAIN: Wouldn't surprise me ... and then we'd be scuppered.

ALICE: It's all your fault. You spoil them. Then they get ideas.

CAPTAIN: I know how to talk to them, you don't. That's the difference between us.

ALICE: You don't talk, you grovel. You do with all inferiors without realising. You might act the bully, but really, inside, you're a slave.

CAPTAIN: Very good!

ALICE: And you grovel with your men. It's only with your equals and superiors that you become the love-sick girl.

CAPTAIN [*as if hurt*]: Ah!

ALICE: Don't bully me! ... do you think Mary'll leave?

CAPTAIN: Yes, unless you talk sweetly to her.

ALICE: Me?

CAPTAIN: Yes. I can't, you'll accuse me of flirting.

ALICE: It'll be unbearable if she goes. Think of the housework, my hands!

CAPTAIN: I can imagine worse. If Mary goes, cook will follow, and we won't get new girls. Either the men on the ferry scare them away, and if they don't manage, my sentries do—

ALICE: Who I feed, and who hang around all day because their CO won't order them out.

CAPTAIN: I can't do that. They'd go AWOL ... who'd man the battery?

ALICE: They're ruining us.

CAPTAIN: Which is why the mess committee asked the War Office for an increased allowance—

ALICE: For us?

CAPTAIN: For the men, daftie.

ALICE [*laughing*]: Daft, yourself.

CAPTAIN: Good ... laugh a bit.

ALICE: I thought I've forgotten.

CAPTAIN [*lighting cigar*]: Don't ever forget to laugh ... it's fatal.

ALICE: Fancy another hand?

CAPTAIN: No. No, I'm tired. [*Pause*]

ALICE: I'm quite put out Conor's gone to our enemies' party before us.

CAPTAIN: Don't bother with him!

ALICE: In the *Times*, on the Kingstown list, Conor was 'a man of independent means'. Do you think he's come in to money?

CAPTAIN: 'Independent means.' Oh, our first rich relation!

ALICE: In your family, maybe. Plenty of rich ones in mine.

CAPTAIN: Now he has money, Conor wants to show off. A common problem, but he shan't fool me. I'll play my cards close to my chest.

[*The telegraph apparatus begins to click.*]

ALICE: Who wants us?

CAPTAIN [*standing still*]: Be quiet!

ALICE: What does it say?

CAPTAIN: If you don't stop I can't hear! It's the children!

[*The* CAPTAIN *walks over to the apparatus and taps out a reply. The apparatus taps back. The* CAPTAIN *taps out an answer.*]

ALICE: And?

CAPTAIN: Hold it. [*The* CAPTAIN *taps the 'message over' signal.*] Judith's sick again. She's off school.

ALICE: Not again! Anything else?

CAPTAIN: No money ... as usual!

ALICE: Why's she working so hard now, she can do the exams next year!

CAPTAIN: You can tell her but she won't listen.

ALICE: You're her father ... you convince her.

CAPTAIN: I tried! Pointless! Children just go their own sweet way—

ALICE: In this family, yes.

[*The* CAPTAIN *yawns.*]

ALICE: Must you yawn?

CAPTAIN: I can help it! I'm so bored by how we repeat ourselves. You said just now, 'In this family,' to which I'd usually reply 'It's not just *my* family. Aren't *you* part of *this family* too?' But I've said that so often I yawned instead which could either mean, 'You're so right,' or, 'Can we stop this, please!'

ALICE: You're so amusing this evening.

CAPTAIN: Is it time to eat yet?

ALICE: You know who's cooking for Haverty? The chef from the Great Northern.

CAPTAIN: I bet grouse is on the menu. Delicious. The world's supreme game bird. Only not if its roasted in lard.

ALICE: Must we talk about their food?

CAPTAIN: Their wine then! What'd'you say those yahoo's are drinking?

ALICE: A little soothing music?

CAPTAIN [*sitting at the desk*]: Why not? But none of your funeral marches or Oirish laments. No need to underline what I can work out. 'My husband's so horrid. Would I was dead.' Roll drums, sound trumpets, take your partners pl ... ease, for 'The Walls of Limerick'. There's champagne in the pantry. Can we open one ... have a party?

ALICE: I bought those bottles and I mean to keep them.

CAPTAIN: Oh! Careful with the pennies!

ALICE: I have to be. You've always been so mean!

CAPTAIN: I can't see how we'll fill the evening ... unless I dance for you.

ALICE: Don't! You're too old.

CAPTAIN: You need a live-in female companion!

ALICE: And a male companion for you!

CAPTAIN: You're too kind. But can I remind you, we did try it ... and at first, dare I say it, we were happy—

ALICE: Look what happened!

CAPTAIN: You're right. Let's drop it.

[*There is a timid knock on the door from the kitchen.*]

ALICE: Who could that be?

CAPTAIN: Mary's started knocking!

ALICE: Don't shout 'Come in!' Go and open the door. This is a house not a barracks.

CAPTAIN [*moving towards the door leading to the kitchen*]: Anything to do with my work, you resent it!

[*There is another knock, bolder.*]

ALICE: Open the door.

[*The* CAPTAIN *opens the door. A hand comes in with a visiting card.*]

CAPTAIN [*to* ALICE]: It's Cook! [*To Cook, off-stage.*] Has Mary deserted us? [*Inaudible reply from off-stage. Turning to* ALICE.] Mary's scarpered.

ALICE: I'm a maid again.

CAPTAIN: And I'm the drudge.

ALICE: Couldn't we have one of your sentries in?

CAPTAIN: That would be rather frowned upon.

ALICE: Hang on, that card couldn't be from Mary, surely it couldn't?

CAPTAIN [*squints at the card through his pince-nez, then hands the card to* ALICE]: I can't ... you read it.

ALICE [*reads*]: Conor! It's Conor! Get out and welcome him!

CAPTAIN [*he goes out the door leading to the kitchen. We hear the* CAPTAIN *off-stage*]: Conor. What a surprise!

[ALICE *tidies her hair. She is bright and alive.*]

CAPTAIN [*returning with* CONOR]: Come on, you old traitor. You sneaked in through the kitchen door but you know you're welcome.

ALICE: Yes, Conor, you know you're welcome.

CONOR: Thank you. How many years, is it?

CAPTAIN: Fifteen, I think. And no doubt it shows. We're older.

ALICE: Not Conor, not at all. Not even a grey hair.

CAPTAIN: Take a pew. First things first. What are your plans? Are you free for dinner?

CONOR: I was asked to Doctor Haverty's. I haven't said 'yes', though.

ALICE: Eat with us then.

CONOR: We're family, and that's what I want to do ... but he is my boss.

CAPTAIN: Ignore him. No boss ever frightened me.

CONOR: I'm not frightened. It's just not going could be awkward later.

CAPTAIN: I rule this island. Fall in with us, and no one will touch you.

ALICE: Thank you, Edgar. [*Taking Conor's hand*] Eat with us. No one will take it amiss. We're family.

CONOR: All right. You've made me feel welcome, certainly.

CAPTAIN: And why wouldn't we? Have we fallen out? [CONOR *is embarrassed.*] You stepped out of line, once, but you were young. I can't even remember the details.

[*Now* ALICE *is embarrassed. The three sit at the sewing table.*]

ALICE: So, you've been out in the world?

CONOR: And now I'm back with you—

CAPTAIN: The couple you married off.

CONOR: Did I? I don't think so. Anyway, I'm impressed, all these years later and you're still together—

CAPTAIN: Yes, that's an achievement. Had our share of bad times, but good ones too. And Alice can't complain. No shortage of money, and perhaps you don't know but, I've had a bit of literary success—

CONOR: Right! Last time we met you'd just published a rifle manual? Is it still used in training?

CAPTAIN: It's in print. The army tried to suppress it but the new manual's such dross, mine marches on.

[*An awkward silence*]

CONOR: And a little bird told me you've been travelling.

ALICE: Yes. Five trips to Paris. Imagine that!

CAPTAIN: Those were her ladyship's terms when I nabbed her—

ALICE: What!

CAPTAIN: When I snatched you from the theatre—

ALICE: I wasn't a fort that you stormed.

CAPTAIN: When I finished her brilliant career, I had to promise to take her to the continent, a promise I kept because I am a gentleman. We've been [*counting on his fingers*] five times. Been to France yourself?

CONOR: No. Portugal, the African colonies ... do they count? ... and New York, of course.

CAPTAIN: I hear it's full of criminals.

CONOR: I'm sure it's nothing like Paris.

ALICE: Tell me ... any word from your children?

CONOR [*abruptly*]: No.

ALICE: Conor, it wasn't exactly smart storming off—

CONOR: I didn't. The Judge awarded custody to their mother.

CAPTAIN: You had a close escape there, but don't talk about it now!

CONOR [*to* ALICE]: What about your little ones?

ALICE: They're fine. At school. And not so little any more.

CAPTAIN: But they're superb. The boy's going to be a first class officer.

ALICE: We don't know yet if the army want him.

CAPTAIN: If? He'll be the Minister of War.

CONOR: On a different tack ... there's a quarantine station coming ... I'll be working with Haverty. What sort of a fellow is he?

CAPTAIN: Ignorant yahoo—

CONOR [*to* ALICE]: Oh, not much fun, eh?

ALICE: The Captain exaggerates as always, but I don't warm to the doctor myself—

CAPTAIN: Answer your cousin's question! Haverty's awful, like everyone here, and that is why I have nothing to do with anyone.

CONOR: You don't get on with anyone?

CAPTAIN: No!

ALICE: As you'll find out, you can't be friends with anyone here.

CAPTAIN: Every bully and bureaucrat in the Kingdom is on this island.

ALICE [*ironically*]: Yes.

CAPTAIN [*amiably*]: Lumping me in with the riff-raff? But I don't throw my weight around the house.

ALICE: You daren't.

CAPTAIN [*to* CONOR]: Pay no attention. Though I say it myself, I'm a fair husband, and she's the best wife in the world.

ALICE: Conor, you must be dying for a drink?

CONOR: No, thanks, I don't.

CAPTAIN: Oh, the Papist's taken the pledge?

CONOR: I just don't like it.

CAPTAIN: American habit?

CONOR: Yes.

CAPTAIN: I've no time for this. A man who can't hold his drink is not a man.

CONOR: Oh, I can. But because of my job I'm going to get tangled up with everyone's problems and I must keep a clear head ... don't you see?

ALICE: Meet them first. Then you'll find your true friends. You're sitting with them.

CONOR: Isn't it miserable ... alone in this tower, only enemies outside?

ALICE: It's certainly no fun.

CAPTAIN: Don't exaggerate. It's not all terrible. My whole life's been one long battle, but everyone who's opposed me helped me; they made me stronger. And when the time comes, I'll leave this earth owing nobody. Everything you see, I earned it. I got nothing for free.

ALICE: His path hasn't been strewn with roses—

CAPTAIN: No, flints and thorns. But my strength got me through, same as you.

CONOR: Strength isn't everything. You've got to bend. I learnt that in the divorce.

CAPTAIN: Then I'm sorry for you.

ALICE: Edgar!

CAPTAIN: I'm sorry for him if he can't rely on his own strength. Look, when the machine stops, what are you? A barrowful of muck, only fit for the garden. But so long as you're alive, you've got to fight and struggle. Sheer effort and a refusal to submit, that's how I got this far.

CONOR [*smiling*]: You're on form tonight.

CAPTAIN: But I speak the truth!

CONOR: I don't think so.

CAPTAIN: Well, that's where you're wrong.

[*During this exchange the music stops, a wind starts and the French doors start to bang.*]

CAPTAIN [*getting up*]: There's a storm brewing.

[*The* CAPTAIN *closes the French doors and taps the barometer.*]

ALICE [*to* CONOR]: You will stay and eat?

CONOR: Yes, thanks.

ALICE: It'll be rough and ready. The maid's run off, but I've still got a cook.

CONOR: Simple suits me.

ALICE: It's wonderful, you're so well-mannered.

CAPTAIN: Amazing how the barometer's fallen. And I felt it.

ALICE [*whispers to* CONOR]: He's very highly strung.

CAPTAIN: When's the grub coming?

ALICE [*getting up*]: I'll see what I can rustle up. You two can sit and talk about higher things. [*Whispers to* CONOR] Agree with everything he says and don't ask why he's not a Major!

[CONOR *nods.* ALICE *goes towards the door to the kitchen.*]

CAPTAIN: Is it going to be edible, tonight, dear?

ALICE: Give me the cash, and it'll be edible.

CAPTAIN: It's always cash. [ALICE *goes out.*] Cash, cash, cash. Day in, day out, my hand's in my wallet. Sometimes I actually think I *am* a wallet.

CONOR: Oh yes, been there.

CAPTAIN: Ah, you too have drunk the bitter cup of matrimony. Damned women! And yours was an ugly specimen—

CONOR [*gently*]: I'd rather not talk about her—

CAPTAIN: I mean a jewel! And mine's not bad for all her failings.

CONOR [*smiles, in a good-natured way*]: For all her failings!

CAPTAIN: What's funny?

CONOR [*still smiling*]: Her failings!

CAPTAIN: She's loyal, an exceptional mother [*He glances at the door to the kitchen.*] but she's got a terrible temper. I've often cursed you for foisting her onto me.

CONOR [*friendly*]: I did nothing of the kind—

CAPTAIN: You did, you've forgotten. But don't think I'm angry, even if I sound it. It's just I shout at soldiers all day and at home I repeat myself.

CONOR: I didn't impose Alice. Quite the opposite.

CAPTAIN [*in full flow, ignoring* CONOR]: Funny how life turns out.

CONOR: I suppose.

CAPTAIN: Getting old ... interesting but not nice. I'm not over the hill but with one acquaintance after the other going down, I feel so alone.

CONOR: Give thanks you have a wife to grow old with.

CAPTAIN: Give thanks? Huh! And the children leave you too, speaking of which, you shouldn't have left yours.

CONOR: I didn't. They were taken.

CAPTAIN: It was horrible but try not to be angry.

CONOR: But what happened isn't what you said.

CAPTAIN: Well ... who cares? ... it's over! Now you're on your own.

CONOR: You can get used to it.

CAPTAIN: Can you? What about being utterly alone?

CONOR: Well, look at me!

CAPTAIN: What have you been doing for the last fifteen years?

CONOR: It's a long time. Where'd you want me to start?

CAPTAIN: Did you inherit money? Are you rich?

CONOR: Not exactly rich—

CAPTAIN: Don't worry. I'm not going to ask for any.

CONOR: You'd be welcome ... I'd be happy to help—

CAPTAIN: I've got quite a large income, thank you. [*The* CAPTAIN *glances at the door to the kitchen.*] But I have to keep a steady flow of cash coming. If it ever dries up ... she walks.

CONOR: Seriously?

CAPTAIN: You've no idea. If money's even a tiny bit tight ... as happens, occasionally ... and she loves to tell me I'm a bad breadwinner.

CONOR: But you just said you've a big income.

CAPTAIN: Yes, but it's never big enough for her ladyship.

CONOR: Then it can't be 'big' in the accepted sense—

CAPTAIN: Sometimes, there's no pleasing some people.

[*The telegraph apparatus begins to tap.*]

CONOR: Is that a message?

CAPTAIN: It's just the time signal.

CONOR: Why no telephone?

CAPTAIN: It's in the kitchen but give me that any day. [*Pointing at the telegraph*] No one can eavesdrop on one of them.

CONOR: Does it drive you mad, living here?

CAPTAIN: Yes, but I'd be the same wherever I was. Now, tell me ... after we die, is there peace then?

CONOR: No, it's all trouble and strife there too.

CAPTAIN: If 'there' exists. Better nothing then.

CONOR: Except, on the way to nothing, there could be a lot of pain.

CAPTAIN: I'm going to die just like that! [*Snaps fingers*]

CONOR: You're sure of that?

CAPTAIN: Yes!

CONOR: You're so unhappy, aren't you?

CAPTAIN [*sighing*]: Unhappy. But the day I go, then I'll be happy.

CONOR: How do you know? The moment hasn't come. Now tell me, what really goes on here? The air is thick with hatred. If I hadn't promised Alice to stay, frankly, I'd go. [*The* CAPTAIN *slides down his chair and stares into the distance.*] Oh, my goodness. [*Shaking the Captain's shoulder*] Edgar!

CAPTAIN [*slowly coming to*]: What? [*The* CAPTAIN *looks around.*] It was Alice speaking, I thought, just now, but it's you ... [*Becomes tranced again.*]

CONOR: This is horrible. [*Going to the door to the kitchen*] Alice!

[ALICE *comes in wearing an apron.*]

ALICE: What is it?

CONOR: He's had some sort of a turn.

ALICE [*serenely*]: Oh, that's nothing. Some music will bring him back.

CONOR: Hold on. I want to look at him. Can he hear? Or see?

ALICE: Course he can't hear. Or see. He's having a fit.

CONOR: You think it's nothing. Alice, what is going on with you two?

ALICE: Ask that lump.

CONOR: That's your husband.

ALICE: No, it's a stranger who slept with me all these years. I know no more about him now than when we started—

CONOR: Quiet, he'll hear.

ALICE: He hears nothing when he's like this.

[*A bugle plays outside.*]

CAPTAIN [*jumps up, takes hat and coat from hook*]: Apologies. Sentry inspection.

[*The* CAPTAIN *hurries out the French doors.*]

CONOR: He's not well.

ALICE: He's worse than usual.

CONOR: His nerves are shot.

ALICE: He's worse than usual.

CONOR: Is he drinking?

ALICE: He pretends he is, but he's not a drinker.

CONOR: Sit and slowly, calmly, tell me the truth.

ALICE [*sitting*]: Where do I begin? My years here were and are a life sentence. I hate the man I married, and my hatred is now so deep, I'll dance with joy the day he dies.

CONOR: Then why not separate?

ALICE: I wish! When we were engaged we broke it off, twice ... and we've tried to break it off every day since we married. We did manage it once ... in here ... five years ago ... but it won't happen again. We're welded together. Only death can prise us apart.

CONOR: You might be inseparable yet you're so alone, aren't you?

ALICE: Completely! He drove my brothers and sisters away, 'rooted' them out he said, like weeds ... and my women friends, everybody—

CONOR: But his relatives ... didn't you 'root' them out in return?

ALICE: Had to! They wanted to chew me up and then spit me out. Now, I'm alone. [*Pointing at the telegraph*] That's my lifeline. Can't use the telephone ... the operators eavesdrop. So I've learnt Morse code, but don't let on to him, for God's sake, or he'll kill me.

CONOR: Appalling! But tell me. Why's Edgar think it's my fault you're married. Surely you remember? Edgar and I were friends, he saw you, fell head over heels in love, pleaded with me to be the go-between. I said no, I knew what a hard-hearted monster you were. I warned him, but, silly Edgar, he persisted, until in the end I told him to get your brother to plead his case.

ALICE: I believe you, but now he's convinced himself you forced me on him, he'll never accept the truth.

CONOR: I see. Well, if it makes him feel any better, he can blame me.

ALICE: You're letting him off lightly—

CONOR: What I really can't stand is how he keeps saying I abandoned my children. He's wrong.

ALICE: But that's him. He lies, and then he ends believing his lies. Yet he really likes you, perhaps because you don't contradict him. And it would mean a great deal to me if you would carry on like this. You couldn't have come at a better time. Your arrival is like the relief of Mafeking. You must help us, somehow.

There isn't another couple as miserable on the face of this earth. [*Weeps*]

CONOR: I saw one marriage at close quarters ... that was bad ... but this is much worse.

ALICE: Is it?

CONOR: Yes!

ALICE: Who do you blame?

CONOR: Alice! My troubles taught me never to blame. You've simply got to accept your lot and often things get better—

ALICE: I shan't. It's unbearable. [*Getting up*] And never ending—

CONOR: Tell me. Why do you hate each other as much as you do?

ALICE: I don't know. There isn't any purpose to it ... we just do. And do you know what frightens him most about his dying? My re-marrying.

CONOR: Which proves he loves you!

ALICE: All right! But he hates me as well.

CONOR [*as if to himself*]: 'Hell born love hatred makes' as my mother would say. Tell me, does he get you to play much for him?

ALICE: Yes, and the gloomier the better, like that horrible 'Ride of the Whiteboys'. He hears that and he wants to dance.

CONOR: Can he, at his age?

ALICE: If the humour's on him.

CONOR: And, if you don't mind me asking, what about your children?

ALICE: You know two died?

CONOR: You've been through that, too?

ALICE: What haven't I been through?

CONOR: What about the other two?

ALICE: Boarding school, Dublin. He poisoned them and now they hate me.

CONOR: But didn't you do the same?

ALICE: Course. But then it got disgusting, Edgar and I canvassing the children, bribing them ... we saw we must send them away, or we'd destroy them. They should have brought us together but they drove us apart. It's so unfair, sometimes I think we're cursed.

CONOR: Well, aren't we, since our first sin?

ALICE [*staring, angrily*]: What?

CONOR: Adam and Eve.

ALICE: Oh, right. I thought you meant something else!

[*There is an embarrassed silence.*]

ALICE [*squeezing his hands*]: Conor, cousin and friend. I haven't always been kind, have I? Well, now I've got my just deserts. Does it give you a sneaking satisfaction?

CONOR: Not at all. Nothing like that.

ALICE: Cast your mind back to a Sunday more than twenty years ago. You were engaged. I asked you to dinner—

CONOR: Stop!

ALICE: When you got to the house, Edgar and I were out—

CONOR: You were invited somewhere ... it doesn't matter now—

ALICE: Conor, listen! When I asked you to eat with us, I thought there was food. [*Hiding her face in her hands*] But there isn't so much as a crust of bread. You must think I'm always offering food and failing you—

CONOR: No, Alice.

ALICE: When *he* gets back, he'll demand his dinner, but I've nothing ... he'll hit the roof. You've never seen one of his rages ... God this is humiliating!

CONOR: Why don't I go off and get something?

ALICE: In a garrison, at this hour! Everything here shuts at four, army regulations.

CONOR: Never mind, I'm not hungry ... Let's think! We've got to joke when he gets back about the cupboard being bare. No, better idea. I'll give him a drink, we'll play some cards, I'll let him win of course—and you'll be waiting at the piano when he comes in ... go on, sit down!

ALICE: I can't play with these. Look! Ragged nails. Cracked skin. You know why? Scrubbing pots, hauling coal, ironing, washing—

CONOR: But you said the maid only just left ... all untrue!—

ALICE: Yes, well, she lies ... which is just typical ... she lies ... they go AWOL all the time ... they hate us ... and then I have to skivvy. How am I going to get out of supper? Wouldn't it be brilliant if this tower burnt down?

CONOR: Alice! Don't tempt fate!

ALICE: Or if the sea rose and drowned us?

CONOR: I don't want to hear any more.

ALICE: You can't go. You must help me. What will I say to him?

CONOR: Alice, I'm not going—

ALICE: But what will I do when you're gone?

CONOR: Does he hit you?

ALICE: Me? No! He's not *that* stupid. It would finish everything and he knows it.

[*Cries off-stage of 'Halt! Who goes there?' 'Friend.'*]

CONOR [*getting up*]: It's himself!

ALICE [*fearfully*]: I'm afraid so. [*Pause*]

CONOR: How should we play this?

ALICE: No idea, don't ask me!

[*The* CAPTAIN *comes through the French doors he went out of earlier. He is smiling and in good humour.*]

CAPTAIN: Duty done ... the evening is mine. Has she turned you against me, Conor? Make a stone weep, she can.

CONOR: What's the weather like?

CAPTAIN [*CHEERFULLY*]: Stormy! [*He opens one of the French doors slightly.*] So, I am Balor of the Baleful Eye, and she is the captive princess, and outside stands my wicked sentry. And here he comes ... left, right, left, right, tee-tum-tee-tum, tee-tum-tee-tum. Shall we do our sword dance, fairest? Conor would like that.

CONOR: No, 'The Ride of the Whiteboys'.

CAPTAIN: You know that? Alice ... never mind the apron ... play!—

[ALICE *sits and the* CAPTAIN *pinches her very hard.*]

CAPTAIN [*to* ALICE]: You've been telling lies about me.

ALICE: Me! [ALICE *plays 'The Ride of the Whiteboys, a wild, malevolent jig. The* CAPTAIN *reaches for a sword from the wardrobe and goes behind the desk where he begins to act out a fight in which he plays both the protagonists. We hear the metal tips of the Captain's boots on the floor. As* ALICE *plays faster, the Captain's movements grow wilder and more feverish. Suddenly, the* CAPTAIN *lets out a groan and falls to the ground, where he lies unnoticed by* CONOR *and* ALICE *who plays on to the end. She continues without looking round.*] Encore, maestro?

[*Silence.* ALICE *looks and sees the* CAPTAIN *lying unconscious on the floor, hidden from the audience by the desk.*] Blessed Jesus!

[ALICE *stands slowly and crosses herself. Then she gives a great sigh of gratitude mixed with satisfaction.*]

CONOR [*hurrying to the* CAPTAIN]: The man's dying.

ALICE [*stonily*]: I hope he's dead. Is he?

CONOR: Instead of gloating, try helping!

ALICE [*without moving*]: I won't touch him ... Is he dead?

CONOR: No, he's breathing.

[ALICE *sighs. The* CAPTAIN *rises slowly.* CONOR *helps him to an armchair. The* CAPTAIN *sits.*]

CAPTAIN: What was that? [*Silence*] What was that?

CONOR: You fell.

CAPTAIN: Where's my sword?

CONOR: You fainted. How do you feel now?

CAPTAIN: How do I feel? ... I feel ... why are you staring at me?

CONOR: You need a doctor.

CAPTAIN: Certainly not. Alice, back to the ivories ... Ah! Here it comes again! [*The* CAPTAIN *clasps his head.*]

ALICE: You're unwell.

CAPTAIN: Stop shouting. I'm just dis ... com ... bob ... ulated.

CONOR: He must see someone. I'll telephone the Doctor.

CAPTAIN: Not bloody Haverty, you hear.

CONOR: The garrison Doctor must see you now.

CAPTAIN: If that sawbones comes here ... I'll shoot him. Ah! [*Cradling his head*] There's the pain again!

CONOR [*going to the door leading to the kitchen*]: I'm going to telephone.

[CONOR *goes.* ALICE *removes her apron.*]

CAPTAIN: Will you get me water!

ALICE: I'll have to!

[*Gets him a glass of water*]

CAPTAIN: How delightful.

ALICE: Are you really ill?

CAPTAIN: I apologise, my attack spoilt your evening.

ALICE: Will I have to nurse you?

CAPTAIN: You don't want to, surely?

ALICE: Why wouldn't I?

CAPTAIN: Because it ... he's come, what you've waited all your married life for!

ALICE: Yes, and you never thought he ... it would come, did you!

CAPTAIN: Don't be angry with me.

CONOR [*coming back*]: It's outrageous ...

ALICE: What?

CONOR: I got through, he wouldn't come to the telephone!

ALICE [*to the* CAPTAIN]: See what you've done? This is Haverty paying
   you back for all your insults.

CAPTAIN: My head is splitting ... get Doctor Flood from Londonderry.

ALICE [*going to telegraph*]: I'll have to telegraph him.

CAPTAIN [*sitting up, surprised*]: You ... telegraph—?

ALICE [*operating the machine*]: Yes, but you've never noticed.

CAPTAIN: Well ... go to it ... deceiver. I see you clearly now. [*To*
   CONOR] You, come. [CONOR *goes over and sits.*] Hold my hand! I
   feel I've tumbled from the battlements and now I'm drowning
   in the sea!

CONOR: Has anything like this ever happened before?

CAPTAIN: Never—

CONOR [*standing*]: It'll take hours to get someone out. I'm going
   to go talk to Haverty and reason with him. He does know you,
   doesn't he?

CAPTAIN: Yes.

CONOR: I mean, he knows your medical history?

   [*The* CAPTAIN *shrugs.* CONOR *goes towards the porch door.*]

ALICE: I'll soon have a reply from the mainland. Thank you,
   Conor! Get back quick.

CONOR: Soon as I can. [CONOR *leaves.*]

CAPTAIN: How nice Conor is. I'd forgotten!

ALICE: Yes, he's greatly improved. But I do feel sorry for him.
   Getting mixed up with us, now.

CAPTAIN: On our silver jubilee! Tell me, how does he really seem
   to you? He never talks about himself. Have you noticed?

ALICE: Yes; but we haven't put any searching questions, have we?

CAPTAIN: God! he's had a life. But so have we. Does everyone live
   like this?

ALICE: Maybe, only they never talk about it!

CAPTAIN: Happy people always attach themselves to happy people
   and avoid catastrophe, whereas we unhappy ones never know
   anything but.

ALICE: Don't you know any happy people?

CAPTAIN: Let me think ... No ... Yes ... The Shillidays!

ALICE: What! She just had that disgusting operation on her ...

CAPTAIN: All right! Can I think of anyone else? ... the Finnegans.

ALICE: Yes. Idyllic family life, money, good position in society,
   children married well. Then their cousin comes home from

Boston, he's arrested in a public convenience, he goes to jail ...
They're on the front page of every newspaper; they can't show
their face in Londonderry. They flee to England where now
they're deeply unhappy living in ... yes, Morden!

CAPTAIN: I wonder what this is?

ALICE: What do you mean?

CAPTAIN: My heart or my head. My soul wants to jump from my
mouth and float away like smoke.

ALICE: Something to eat?

CAPTAIN: Yes! What's for dinner?

ALICE [*walking dejectedly across the room*]: I'll ask Mary.

CAPTAIN: She's gone.

ALICE: Yes, yes, yes!

CAPTAIN: Get cook. I want fresh water.

ALICE [*ringing bell*]: Can you believe it ... ! [*Ringing again*] No
answer.

CAPTAIN: Go and look ... God, think if she's left as well!

ALICE [*going to the door to the kitchen*]: Would you believe it? Cook's
trunk is packed and in the corridor.

CAPTAIN: So, she's gone too!

ALICE: I can't stand it ... [*Starting to cry, sinks down onto her knees, puts
her face on the seat of a chair, and sobs.*]

CAPTAIN: Trouble never comes in a single platoon but always in
battalions. Our lowest point ever and Conor chooses this time
to visit!

ALICE: He's gone too, you know, and he's not coming back!

CAPTAIN: Nothing would surprise me.

ALICE: It's all over ...

CAPTAIN: Meaning?

ALICE: We've the plague, no one will come near us now.

CAPTAIN: To hell with them. [*The telegraph starts tapping.*] Hah! Stop
rustling your skirts ... 'Regret. No doctor available.' None! It's
a boycott.

ALICE: Not a doctor in the county'll treat you ... you never pay your
bills.

CAPTAIN: That's a lie ...

ALICE: Even when you have money, you don't pay. Because you
hold them in the same contempt as you hold ... everyone in my
profession. You think everyone and everything in the world is

useless apart from your precious batteries of 4.2 howitzers or whatever they are and your bolt action rifles!

CAPTAIN: Pretty little lecture ...

ALICE: You reap what you sow!

CAPTAIN: Oh, it's a sermon?

ALICE: You dug this hole. When was cook last paid? Six months ago!

CAPTAIN: Yes, since when she has been stealing her wages.

ALICE: And I, meanwhile, have been borrowing from her.

CAPTAIN: That doesn't surprise me!

ALICE: She never stole and that money I borrowed was so the children could come home on holiday.

CAPTAIN: Conor's gutless. Couldn't come clean and say, 'I'm off to Haverty's party. It'll be more fun than yous two.' No, he had to sneak away pretending he's getting help! He hasn't changed.

CONOR [*rushing in*]: Edgar ... I've ... uh ... some quite good news mostly. Doctor Haverty says he knows all about your heart ... in fact everyone at the party knew about it—

CAPTAIN: My heart?

CONOR: There's a hardening—

CAPTAIN: Hardening?

CONOR: Well ...

CAPTAIN: Is it life threatening?

CONOR: Yes, at some stage ...

CAPTAIN: It's life threatening?

CONOR: Yes.

CAPTAIN: So, I'm dead.

CONOR: Unless you're careful. No cigars. [*Holding up the cigar the* CAPTAIN *was smoking earlier*] No whiskey. Straight up to bed.

CAPTAIN [*fearful*]: Not *that* bed I'm not! Once I'm there I'm finished. Over. I'll kip on the sofa tonight. Did Haverty say anything else?

CONOR: He was cordial. He said if you need him you only have to ask.

CAPTAIN: Cordial, was he? The fake! I don't want to see him. Can I eat?

CONOR: He said milk only.

CAPTAIN: Milk!

CONOR: For a few days.

CAPTAIN: An old woman's drink.

CONOR: You'll get to like it.

CAPTAIN: Not at my time of life. [*Clutching head*] Ah! the pain.
  [*The* CAPTAIN *stares ahead, blankly.*]

ALICE [to CONOR]: What exactly did Haverty say?

CONOR: He may die.

ALICE: What news!

CONOR: Careful, Alice! Go and get some blankets and pillows.
  We'll put him on the sofa. I'll sleep here tonight, keep an eye
  on him.

ALICE: And me?

CONOR: Go to bed. He's much worse when you're around.

ALICE: Order and I obey. You want to help us, don't you?
  [ALICE *goes towards the door to the kitchen.*]

CONOR: I want to help you *both*. I'm not taking sides.
  [ALICE *has left before* CONOR *finishes speaking.* CONOR *picks up the
  empty water jug and goes out after* ALICE. *The wind rises and the door
  leading to the porch blows open; so does the front door. An* OLD WOMAN
  creeps in. Her feet are bare.]

CAPTAIN [*waking*]: Abandoned me, have they? Typical. [*Looking
  around he sees the* OLD WOMAN *and is startled.*] Who are you? What
  do you want?

OLD WOMAN: I came in simply to close the doors, kind sir.

CAPTAIN: Why?

OLD WOMAN: Wind pushed 'em open at the very instant I was
  passing.

CAPTAIN: Liar. You came in to steal.

OLD WOMAN: I know from Mary there's nothing here worth the
  taking.

CAPTAIN: Mary?

OLD WOMAN: Good night, your honour, sleep well.
  [*The* OLD WOMAN *goes out, closing the porch and the front door after
  herself.* ALICE *comes in with bedding through the door from the kitchen.*]

CAPTAIN: Who was that just now?

ALICE: Old Eileen from the laundry. She was just walking by.

CAPTAIN: Are you sure?

ALICE: You look terrified!

CAPTAIN: Me? Ludicrous idea.

ALICE: Since you won't go to bed, lie down there.

CAPTAIN [*hobbles to the chaise-longue and lies down*]: I prefer to be here. [*He reaches out for Alice's hand; she pulls it away.* CONOR *comes in carrying the water jug.*] Thank God! You won't leave me, will you?

CONOR: I won't but Alice is going to bed.

CAPTAIN: Good night, Alice.

ALICE: Good night, Conor.

CONOR: Good night.

[ALICE *goes.* CONOR *drags a chair to the chaise-longue and sits.*]

CONOR: Won't you take off your boots?

CAPTAIN: I'm a soldier, I must be ready for action at all times.

CONOR: Kaiser's coming, is he?

CAPTAIN: Maybe. He's coming one day soon. [*Sitting up*] Conor, you are the only person in the world I can ask. If, *when*, I die, look after my children?

CONOR: Why wouldn't I?

CAPTAIN: That's a comfort. Thank you.

CONOR: Why do you trust me?

CAPTAIN: We're not friends, but then I don't believe in friendship. Our families always loathed each other—

CONOR: So why trust me?

CAPTAIN: I don't know, I just do. [*Silence*]

CAPTAIN: Am I going to die?

CONOR: Like all the rest of us. There's no exception being made for you.

CAPTAIN: Are you bitter?

CONOR: Yes. Does it terrify you ... death? ... the wheelbarrow of muck?

CAPTAIN: What if it isn't the end?

CONOR: Well, many think it isn't.

CAPTAIN: And if they're right?

CONOR: We're in for a surprise.

CAPTAIN: We really don't know what awaits us.

CONOR: No, we have to be ready to face anything.

CAPTAIN: Even hell? Or is it only you Catholics who believe in that?

CONOR: I'm surprised you don't, you're already living in hell.

CAPTAIN: Not literally.

CONOR: Come on, what I've seen tonight, this is hell. [*Silence*]

CAPTAIN: You have no idea how I'm torn ápart.

CONOR: Literally?

CAPTAIN: Not the body.

CONOR: Oh, these are spiritual torments. There isn't a third kind, is there? [*Pause*]

CAPTAIN [*standing*]: I can't die.

CONOR: I thought you said you wanted to.

CAPTAIN: So long as it doesn't hurt, I might.

CONOR: Oh, but I think it does.

CAPTAIN: So if this hurts now, that's the start of it then?

CONOR: Yes.

CAPTAIN: Good night to you, so.

CONOR: Good night.

[*As both men stare ahead, wide awake and no likelihood of falling asleep, curtain.*]

SCENE 2

The same, the following morning. The lamp has burnt all night and is spluttering for want of oil. Through the French doors we see the gun battery, a grey sky, the sea, and the SENTRY. *The* CAPTAIN *lies asleep on the chaise-longue, and* CONOR, *awake, sprawls in the armchair nearby. He looks pale, rumpled, unslept.*

ALICE [*coming in*]: Is his lordship sleeping?

CONOR: Since the sun rose.

ALICE: How was last night?

CONOR: Grotesque. He kept me awake with his mad talk.

ALICE: About what?

CONOR: Religion, our purpose here on earth ... schoolboy stuff. As dawn came, he decided the soul is immortal.

ALICE: His own, presumably?

CONOR: What an egomaniac. 'I am, therefore there is a God' ... the creed according to Edgar Dawson.

ALICE: Ah, the penny's dropped with you, has it? Look at those boots! He's stamped on many a heart and soul in those, many a flower and field. And he'd have ground the whole world underfoot given half a chance. Well, now the boot's on my foot!

CONOR: He'd be funny if he wasn't tragic, but for all that he's a weasel, there's something admirable about him, wouldn't you say?

ALICE [*sitting*]: I wouldn't say it even if I thought it. Any praise and his arrogance increases.

[ALICE *covers her mouth with a hand in alarm.*]

CONOR: He can't hear. I gave him enough morphine for an elephant.

ALICE: His family were poor, his father useless. They came down to Dublin and Edgar started work at fourteen. He taught ... very well, not that the family noticed! I first saw him when I was a girl ... winter, ice on the Liffey three inches thick. He was walking to school ... he'd no coat, though the rest of his family had! He was going to teach all day in a room with no fire. His will-power was wonderful, but he was hideous. He frightened me. And he's still hideous, isn't he?

CONOR: Ireland's Quasimodo, and especially ugly when he argues. That's what I remember from our old quarrels. And over the years that horrible face has grown in my imagination. It literally haunted me.

ALICE: Then think what it's been like for me! In his first years the other officers called him Captain Ug, for ugly. They were vile ... he ignored them. Occasionally the Colonel said something and life would improve, not that Edgar ever said thank you. He's good at taking.

CONOR: Really, we should feel sorry for him.

ALICE: Once he's dead ... until then, never!

CONOR: Do you think he's evil?

ALICE: Yes. He can be amusing, and touch your heart if he wishes, but he's a monster.

CONOR: Why was he never made a Major?

ALICE: Think! He's a proven tyrant, he's impossible to promote. But never mention this. He believes he chose to remain a Captain so he could be close to the men ... Did he talk about the children?

CONOR: He wants Judith. He telegraphed the school earlier.

ALICE: I can believe that ... she's his double! He's trained her to hate me. Can you imagine, my own daughter, raised her hand against me?

CONOR: I can't believe that.

ALICE: He's waking! Could he have heard? He's sly ... he could have been pretending to sleep. It's the devil himself. [*Silence*]

CAPTAIN [*rising to his feet and gazing round*]: At last, morning has broken.

CONOR: How's the form?

CAPTAIN: Terrible.

CONOR: Shall I call the doctor?

CAPTAIN: God no! It's Judith I want.

CONOR: Is that sensible? First, shouldn't you put your affairs in order, as we discussed last night ... in case—

CAPTAIN: Of what?

CONOR: What happens to us all.

CAPTAIN: I won't go easy and I'm not ready yet. Alice, you'll have to keep that black dress a few years more—

CONOR: Don't be a typical Irishman ... leave her your furniture ... make a will ... you're not immortal!

CAPTAIN: Give it all to *her* now, are you saying?

CONOR: No. Think! These are married quarters ... you go, she's out. Surely the wife who's cared for all this for twenty-five years has rights to it. I could get a solicitor over this morning.

CAPTAIN: No.

CONOR: You really are an inconsiderate man, aren't you?

CAPTAIN [*grasping head*]: There's the pain again!

ALICE: Do you hear someone at the front door?

CONOR: Was there? Go and see. There's nothing you can do here. [ALICE *goes out to the porch and opens the front door. There is no one there. Then, seeing the* CAPTAIN *has revived, Alice goes out, closing the front door behind.*]

CAPTAIN [*waking*]: So is the new Quarantine Officer going to cope?

CONOR: He'll cope.

CAPTAIN: Between the Colonel and this island lies a strip of water. Don't forget ... I'm king here! You deal with me!

CONOR: Ever go through a quarantine?

CAPTAIN: Before you were born! And let me give you some free advice. Don't put the incinerators near the sea.

CONOR: I was actually—

CAPTAIN: Which shows your ignorance. Germs love water like a pig loves filth. It's their element.

CONOR: But salt water is a natural disinfectant!

CAPTAIN: Ignoramus! ... When you've got your quarters sorted, you must get your children across.

CONOR: Do you think they'd come?

CAPTAIN: Yes, if you're man enough. And it'll go down well here, you know ... show the garrison you believe in doing your duty.

CONOR: I've always done my duty!

CAPTAIN [*raising voice*]: That's a matter of opinion, isn't it!

CONOR: I thought I made it—

CAPTAIN [*at the top of his voice*]: It didn't look good, abandoning wife and two—

CONOR: Oh, that's my story, is it?

CAPTAIN: As a senior member through marriage of the same family, I'm going to tell you the truth ... and you'll just have to lump it—

CONOR: Some breakfast?

CAPTAIN: Yes, now you mention it—

CONOR: A lightly boiled egg, perhaps?

CAPTAIN: Invalid food. I want bacon, sausage, blood pudding.

CONOR: It'll kill you.

CAPTAIN: It's not enough I'm ill, you want to starve me as well?

CONOR: No, it's just the way it is.

CAPTAIN: No drink and tobacco either? Life's not worth living!

CONOR: Give them up, and you live a few years more .

ALICE [*coming through the door from the porch with a bunch of wild flowers and a handful of letters and telegrams*]: All for you. [*Throws flowers on the desk.*]

CAPTAIN [*taking post, delighted*]: Really ... I am popular this morning—

ALICE: Only with NCO's and junior officers—

CAPTAIN: You're jealous?

ALICE [*indicating flowers*]: If they were laurel wreaths for academic achievement I might be, but those you'll never get.

CAPTAIN: Hm! ... telegram from Colonel Beggs. Conor could you read it? He's a gentleman, but really, so stupid! Oh! ... this one's from Judith. [*Giving it to* CONOR] Send her a reply at once; I want her here now. Hm! ... another telegram ... I do have friends after all, and it seems I'm about to enjoy some long overdue recognition—

ALICE: What, for being ill?

CAPTAIN: Nasty!

ALICE [*to* CONOR]: I'm reminded of the gunnery officer so loathed ... this was years ago ... the garrison only threw him a party *after* he'd left.

CAPTAIN: Put the flowers in water. [*Opens and reads a third telegram*] I'm not easily taken in and I'm hardly enamoured of the human race, but, by God! this comes from the heart. It could come from nowhere else.

ALICE: Fool.

CONOR [*putting down the Colonel's telegram, reading Judith's*]: Judith can't come. She can't take the time off school.

CAPTAIN: Is that it?

CONOR: Yes ... actually no.

CAPTAIN: Spit it out.

CONOR: She wants you to cut down on your drinking.

CAPTAIN: Incredible! My princess turns out to be a bossy, interfering—

ALICE: It takes one to know one.

CAPTAIN: Is this the best life has to offer because if it is, it's shit!

ALICE: It's your doing! You made her like this! You turned her against me; now she's turning against you. Perhaps there is a God, after all.

CAPTAIN [*to* CONOR]: What does the Colonel say?

CONOR: A months leave, starting today.

CAPTAIN: Leave! I didn't ask for any.

ALICE: No, I did ... while you were sleeping.

CAPTAIN: I won't accept it.

ALICE: You don't have a choice.

CAPTAIN: I certainly do.

ALICE: You see, this is it, Conor, a perfect illustration. My husband ... he doesn't believe in rules, he just does what he pleases. He's the sun, and we're the planets orbiting around him. My husband ... Captain on a godforsaken garrison off the Irish coast ... out of the whole Empire this was the only posting that could be found for him ... Crookedstone, the final resting place of all incompetents. But even the dross out here know him for what he is, a prig, frightened of the dark, selfish, stupid, and a know-all. [*Imitating* EDGAR] 'At the end all yous are's a barrowful of muck and not top notch stuff either.' My husband!

CAPTAIN [*fanning himself with the flowers*]: Did you ask Conor to lunch?

ALICE: No.

CAPTAIN: Go to the kitchen and grill your two best steaks.

ALICE: Two.

CAPTAIN: One for me, one for Conor.

ALICE: We're three.

CAPTAIN: Oh, you want to eat as well ... ah! Make it three. Liberty Hall!

ALICE: Where's the steak coming from? You invited him to supper yesterday evening ... not a crust in the house. He sat up all night on an empty stomach ... no tea this morning ... we haven't any! And our credit's been cancelled at the shop.

CAPTAIN [*to* CONOR]: She's only like this because I didn't die last night.

ALICE: No, because you didn't die twenty-five years ago. Because you weren't dead before I was born.

CAPTAIN: Conor, this is what happens when *you* match-make. A marriage that is not made in heaven, as you see.

[ALICE *and* CONOR *look at one another.*]

CAPTAIN: Nevertheless! No point complaining when there's work to do. [*The* CAPTAIN *pulls on the tunic jacket of his service uniform, a Sam Browne belt with holster, a greatcoat and a peaked khaki cap. He lurches towards the porch door.* ALICE *and* CONOR *block him. The* CAPTAIN *shows holster*]: Yous two can sit on your arses. Get out of my way.

[ALICE *and* CONOR *step aside. The* CAPTAIN *leaves by the porch.*]

ALICE: Go, away with you then. Run away from the truth as you always do, and I'll cover as I always do. You lying, drunken, show-off—

[ALICE *closes the porch door.*]

CONOR: It's never ending.

ALICE: This is nothing. You should see him on a bad day.

CONOR: It gets worse?

ALICE: It can.

CONOR: Where's he get his strength? And where's he off to?

ALICE: Good question. Down to the mess ... he'll thank the junior officers for the flowers, take breakfast with them, drink beer. These are the men he calls 'the filth'. The Colonel's warned him about his attitude ... but he won't listen ... *plus* the Colonel pities him. Of course Edgar thinks the Colonel's scared of him ... As for the wretched wives of the junior officers, Edgar hates them even more than their husbands!

CONOR: When I applied to be Q.M., I hoped to find some peace here ... I never thought things would have got so bad between you two—

ALICE: Dear Conor ... what are you going to do for food?

CONOR: Haverty can give me something ... but what about you? I could get something sent up?

ALICE: No ... Edgar'd kill me if he thought Haverty'd fed me.

CONOR [*looking through the French doors*]: Look at him out there ... in this wind ... amazing.

ALICE: I suppose you have to feel sorry for him ... he can't help himself.

CONOR: I feel for you both ... but what can be done?

ALICE: I don't know. Look! ... He didn't open the bills that came.

CONOR: Isn't it sometimes better not to know?

[*The* CAPTAIN *appears on the battlements outside.*]

ALICE: Look at him now! ... coat open, chest to the wind. He must really want to die!

CONOR: Last night, as his own life was slipping, I felt he wanted to grab mine. Wanted to know everything about me. I had the idea that if he could, he'd have climbed inside my body and lived my life.

ALICE: Yes, that's him, the vampire ... who sucks everything out of everyone because he's got nothing himself. Don't forget this Conor ... keep him out of your house, your life, never tell him your business, or introduce him to your friends. He'll take them and make them his ... he has a special talent for it. But above all, never let him meet your children, or he will become the father to whom they'll turn for advice and help. He will mould them in his image and he'll block your every instruction.

CONOR: Did he have anything to do with what happened with my children—

ALICE: You'll find out in the end so you might as well know now ... yes.

CONOR: I always felt he was mixed up in my business ... I just couldn't be certain.

ALICE: You asked him to go to your wife and mediate. He did the opposite. He told her how to get custody.

CONOR: How stupid of me!

ALICE: I'm surprised you never spotted it.

[*Silence*]

CONOR: You know ... last night, when he was at his lowest ... I had to promise I would never forget his children after he was gone.

ALICE: Do you want to get your own back through my children?

CONOR: No.

ALICE: But you have a beautiful opportunity for revenge.

CONOR: I don't think so.

ALICE: There's nothing he hates more ... nothing ... than generosity of spirit.

CONOR: Ah! The revenge of the decent!

ALICE: Yes ... and in the process evil is punished.

CONOR: Is that what you really want?

ALICE: Yes ... and I always shall ... and the day I forgive my enemy, [*pointing outside*] you can hang me from that gun.

CONOR: If you don't bend soon, you'll break. Hold your tongue, turn the blind eye ... it's called charity. We all need it.

ALICE: I don't. My motto has always been *Fight, fight, fight!*

CONOR: You're not blameless in this.

ALICE: I am. Is there a suffering, known or unknown, that he hasn't inflicted on me, this man I never loved?

CONOR: Why did you marry him then?

ALICE: I was swept off my feet! I was seduced. I wanted to get on in the world.

CONOR: But why leave the theatre?

ALICE: Because I thought one didn't 'do' theatre where I was going. He promised me the world, but what did I get? ... debts! The only gold I ever saw was on his dress uniform and that was as fake as himself.

CONOR: But when men fall in love they mean what they say ... I promised my wife all sorts of things that didn't happen, but that doesn't make me a charlatan ... What are you looking at that's so interesting?

ALICE [*looking through French doors*]: I thought he'd fallen.

CONOR: Has he?

ALICE: No such luck. Well, this won't be the last time he cheats me.

CONOR: I'd better go and find Doctor Haverty.

ALICE [*sitting*]: Off you go Conor, I'm going to sit down and wait. If there's one thing I've learnt, it's how to wait.

ACT TWO

SCENE 1

As before, a few days later. Through the French doors we see the SENTRY. ALICE *sits in an armchair. Her hair is no longer pinned up but hangs down, gathered in a net; it is shot through with streaks of grey.*

CONOR [*coming in from the porch*]: Top of the mornin' Alice.

ALICE: Good morning. Sit down!

CONOR: The ferry's coming into the harbour.

ALICE: Bearing himself, worst luck.

CONOR: What was he doing on the mainland?

ALICE: That's easy. He took his dress uniform and his evening dress. First, the Colonel, then a party.

CONOR: He was so calm the day before yesterday. He doesn't drink and he's a new man, quiet, thoughtful—

ALICE: Imagine what a menace he'd have been if he hadn't drunk all his life. Really, I should be grateful to the whiskey!

CONOR: He was tamed by the bottle ... true ... but have you noticed? ... since his brush with death, he's nicer—

ALICE: No! ... don't believe it. Underneath he's just the same ... a born liar and a schemer!

CONOR [*looking at* ALICE]: Your heart's grown bitter, Alice, and your hair's gone grey.

ALICE: It's been grey for years ... only this morning, I thought, why hide it, my husband's dead ... [*Wildly*] I've lived in this fortress twenty five years. Did you know Fenians were held here?

CONOR: A prison as well as a fortress ... I should have guessed.

ALICE: My complexion would have told you if you'd bothered to look. My children had the prison pallor, as well.

CONOR: I can't imagine this room filled with children's laughter.

ALICE: Two died for want of light ... the survivors never played.

CONOR: What'll happen when he returns?

ALICE: Something nasty. Judith telling him to knock the drink on the head ... that got under his skin. But he can't get back at her, she's out of range, so he's set his sights ... transferred his hatred ... to you.

CONOR: And what exactly is he planning?

ALICE: That's difficult. He has a talent for rooting out people's secrets. And how could you fail to notice that the minute he stopped drinking ... he locked on to you and asked question after question. He could play you now. Amazing. But he's not an actor ... he's a dead man who lives by consuming others ... a cannibal—

CONOR: My thoughts entirely. He's passed across but the corpse doesn't know it. He's got a sort of phosphorescent glow to him, rotting skin, gleaming eyes like will-o'-the-wisp on the bog. And speak of the devil here he comes. Do you think he's jealous?

[*The* CAPTAIN *is on the battlements outside, walking towards the French doors.*]

ALICE: No ... he's far too proud ... 'The *great* have no need of envy precisely because they are great,' ... a favourite saying of his.

CONOR: Well, at least his vices have that advantage. Shall I go out and greet him?

ALICE: No, don't. When he comes in be brusque ... otherwise he'll think you're plotting something. He'll lie ... you nod ... make him think you believe him. Once he goes, I'll tell you what he's up to. Something horrible's coming ... I feel it ... but what ever happens, stay calm. During my quarter-century of war he was always drunk, I was always sober. Whiskey was his Achilles' heel, but not anymore. We must take care.

[*Wearing his dress uniform, the* CAPTAIN *comes through French doors; he is very pale and sick-looking. He stumbles and collapses onto the nearest chair. During the exchange that follows, the* CAPTAIN *holds his sword between his knees.*]

CAPTAIN: Good morning. Forgive me for flopping down. I feel rather faint suddenly.

ALICE & CONOR: Well, good morning.

ALICE: How are we feeling?

CAPTAIN: Fine, just *un peu fatigué*.

ALICE: Any news?

CAPTAIN: The odd trifle. Went to see Dr. Flood who pronounced me fit as a fiddle. Got twenty years to run if I don't indulge.

ALICE [*to* CONOR]: Absolute nonsense. [*To* CAPTAIN] Oh, that is a relief!

CAPTAIN: Yes, I thought so!

[*Silence. The* CAPTAIN *is waiting for the others to speak.*]

ALICE [*to* CONOR]: What ever you do, say nothing. Let him show his hand first.

CAPTAIN [*to* ALICE]: What was that?

ALICE: Nothing ... I didn't say anything.

CAPTAIN [*cautiously*]: Conor, old friend.

ALICE [*to* CONOR]: Watch ... here he goes!

CAPTAIN: Yes, I was in town, you know! [CONOR *nods slowly.*] I was out at the training depot ... they're using my manual ... I met several cadets including ... [*uncertainly*] ... one who's interested in artillery. [*Silence.* CONOR *looks unhappy.*] Well, to cut a long story short, Colonel Beggs said he could come out here and I should prepare him for Woolwich ... Well, don't look so glum. It's Aidan, your son—

ALICE [*to* CONOR]: Vampire ... told you.

CONOR: I should be pleased but I'm not and I won't pretend I am.

CAPTAIN: I don't follow!

CONOR: You don't have too. All you need to know is my answer ... No.

CAPTAIN: But it's too late to close the stable door ... the horse has bolted. He's on his way and he'll be under my command.

CONOR: He can go to another regiment.

CAPTAIN: Sorry, it doesn't work quite like that.

CONOR: Oh yes it does ... I'm his father.

CAPTAIN: Maybe ... but his mother's the one with custody.

CONOR: I'll go to her then.

CAPTAIN: No point.

CONOR: Why?

CAPTAIN: I've already been. Sorry.

[CONOR *tries to stand, fails.*]

ALICE [*to* CONOR]: You must kill him.

CONOR: But he's killed me.

CAPTAIN: That's that settled. [*To* ALICE] What did you just say?

ALICE: Nothing. Your ears are going ... like your eyes!

CAPTAIN: Yes ... Come here ... I've got a secret to tell you!

ALICE: No secrets! Anything you want to say must be witnessed.

CAPTAIN: Good idea, a witness ... and that reminds me ... is the will ready?

ALICE [*hands the* CAPTAIN *a document*]: The solicitor drafted this.

CAPTAIN [*reading*]: Everything to you ... you must be happy, Alice! [*Carefully tearing the will into pieces which he scatters across the carpet.*] But it doesn't make me happy.

ALICE [*to* CONOR]: Have you ever seen his like?

CONOR: He's not human!

CAPTAIN: Now, I have something to tell you, Alice—

ALICE [*anxiously*]: What?

CAPTAIN [*sanguine, as before*]: Given your often expressed desire to put our unhappy marriage out of its misery, given your complete inability to show warmth towards myself or the children, and given the incompetence with which you've managed our affairs, I took the momentous step during my visit of arranging a petition for our divorce.

ALICE: Any reason, dear?

CAPTAIN: Apart from those I just listed, they're all personal. I have twenty years to live and it is my intention to swop my present partner for a woman who will bring affection, youth and who knows? perhaps even a hint of beauty into my life.

ALICE [*ripping off her ring and flinging it into the Captain's lap*]: As you wish.

CAPTAIN [*picking up the ring and slipping it into his pocket*]: Temper, temper. Threw away her ring. I hope my witness has seen!

ALICE [*growing angrier*]: You really intend to throw me out and import another woman into my house?

CAPTAIN: Absolutely.

ALICE: I can play as rough as you ... rougher. Conor, this man tried to kill me.

CONOR: How?

ALICE: He threw me in the sea!

CAPTAIN: Any witnesses? I don't think so—

ALICE: He's lying ... Judith—

CAPTAIN: What's that got to do with it?

ALICE: She'll testify.

CAPTAIN: No, she won't ... she saw nothing.

ALICE: You made her a liar.

CAPTAIN: No, I didn't. You're the actress, the professional liar. You
   did.

ALICE [*realising suddenly*]: You saw Judith, yesterday? She came up
   on the train.

CAPTAIN: Oh yes.

ALICE: God! GOD!

CAPTAIN: The white flag's up, I'll take that as a surrender. [*Takes out
   fob watch, opens it, puts it on the table.*] You have ten minutes to
   leave the garrison ... [*The* CAPTAIN *doubles up as if he has been
   punched.*]

ALICE [*sweeping over and taking his arm*]: What is it?

CAPTAIN: Can't tell.

ALICE: Can I do anything? Do you want a drink?

CAPTAIN: Whiskey? You think I want to die? [*Straightening himself*]
   Take your hands off me. You have ten minutes to evacuate your
   forces. Stragglers can expect no mercy. [*The* CAPTAIN *draws his
   sword.*] Ten minutes!

   [*The* CAPTAIN *marches out through the French doors and along the
   battlement to the* SENTRY.]

CONOR: He's unbelievable

ALICE: He's not a man, he's a monster.

CONOR: And what's this with my son?

ALICE: He's a hostage ... and he'll use Aidan to control you while
   he turns the garrison against you. Do you know what we call this
   place? ... 'Hell's Island'.

CONOR: You're the first woman I've ever felt the slightest bit sorry
   for ... all the others got what they deserved.

ALICE: Then stay ... or he'll beat me, as he has every day of our
   marriage. He beat me in front of the children. He even threw
   me in the sea—

CONOR: That's it, my mind's made up, I can't be his friend. When
   I first came, I was willing to forget the hurt he'd caused, and the
   vile things he'd said. I even forgave him when you told me he'd
   helped my ex-wife to steal my children. But now that he wants
   my son ... I'm sorry, he's beyond the Pale.

ALICE: Boom! I have gunpowder. We'll blow him and this fortress
   to smithereens, even if it means we go down with him. No
   surrender!

CONOR: When I first came here, your hatred was so ... strong, I ...

I wanted to run. But now I have a duty to hate him. The
question is ... what do I do?

ALICE: Identify his enemies ... make them our allies ... just as he
would.

CONOR: I'm amazed he tracked down my wife. It's a shame they
didn't meet twenty-five years ago. That would have been a
match made in hell.

ALICE: Edgar has a weak spot ... I've known for years ... now we
strike—

CONOR: So who's his worst enemy?

ALICE: McBride.

CONOR: Who?

ALICE: The Quartermaster. He knows what Edgar and Sergeant-
Major Hibbert have been 'up' to.

CONOR: Which is?

ALICE: Liberating supplies, selling them on. Embezzlement! This
will ruin him!

CONOR: And you would . . but no, that's not what I want ... no—

ALICE: Afraid to get up close and kill him!

CONOR: Once I might have done so happily but not now.

ALICE: Why?

CONOR: I've learnt that justice always conquers in the end.

ALICE: And you'll wait, will you? Even if your son's stolen ... I might
be grey but just feel the weight of that hair, it's beautiful body.
If Edgar's re-marrying ... why can't I? I know what to do ... one
word from me, I can have him arrested. [ALICE *stamps on the
ground.*] Then I'll dance 'The Ride of Whiteboys' ... on his face.
[ALICE *dances around the room, heaving with laughter.*] Locked in
his dark cell he'll hear the piano as I play ... [ALICE *bangs three or
four notes on the piano.*] And the sentry will no longer be
guarding me but him ... ta-rah-rah-tum-tee-ay, ta-rah-rah-tum-
tee-ay—!

CONOR [*amazed*]: Are you a devil like him?

ALICE [*jumping on a chair, removing a laurel wreath from her portrait,
putting it on*]: I'll wear my crown of triumph on the march to
freedom. They're dusty but they're evergreen, like myself. I'm
not old, Conor!

CONOR [*attracted*]: You are a devil!

ALICE: Yes ... and this is Hell's Island. [*Unbuttoning dress*] I must change. Then we will set in motion his arrest [*indicating the* CAPTAIN] then pouf—!

CONOR [*smiling, lasciviously*]: Alice ... you're a devil!

ALICE: When we were children, you always said we'd marry. Remember? And I said yes. [ALICE *laughs.*] You were so shy then—

CONOR: Alice!

ALICE: Verging on the timid ... but it suited. There are wild women who like retiring types and retiring types who like wild women. You always liked me ... even right back then ... raucous as I was—

CONOR: I don't know you any more.

ALICE: Once an actress, but always a woman, indifferent to convention, free at last ... Turn round, I wish to change.

[ALICE *strips off her dress.* CONOR *throws his arms around* ALICE *and bites her throat. She lets out a shocking scream. The* CAPTAIN *looks back through the French doors.* CONOR *drops* ALICE *onto the sofa and bolts out to the porch and then through the front door. The* CAPTAIN *does not move.*]

SCENE 2

That evening, the same. The SENTRY *is at his post. The laurel wreaths hang over the back of a chair. On the wind-up gramophone, Count John McCormack sings 'Danny Boy'. As the scene plays, the record gets slower and slower.*

The CAPTAIN *is pale and tired-looking with stubble on his chin. He has changed from his dress back to his service uniform. He sits at the desk playing Patience. Suddenly the* CAPTAIN *starts as if he has just heard something. The* CAPTAIN *stares around the room. Nothing.*

The CAPTAIN *returns to his game. He tries to make his cards come out right. They won't. Exasperated, the* CAPTAIN *gathers his cards, goes out to the French doors and flings them over the battlements outside.*

The CAPTAIN *goes to the wardrobe. The wind blows. The French doors bang and make him jump. The* CAPTAIN *stares around the room then extracts three whiskey bottles hidden at the very back of the wardrobe. The* CAPTAIN *goes to the French doors and throws the bottles over the battlements.*

The CAPTAIN *gathers up his boxes of cigars and throws them after the bottles. The* SENTRY *sees everything but does not react.*

The CAPTAIN *takes his glasses off, polishes the lenses with a handkerchief, then tests them to see how well he sees with them. Useless. He throws the spectacles out through the French doors and over the battlements, then stumbles across the room to the desk, on top of which stands a candelabra. By using his fingers to feel what he is doing, he lights the six candles in the candelabra.*

As he blows out the match, the CAPTAIN *notices the laurel wreath on the back of the chair. He picks up the wreath and turns towards the French doors. Then he thinks better of what he is about to do. He cleans the wreath with the cloth draped over the piano then hangs it back on the portrait of Alice.*

The CAPTAIN *goes to the piano. He punches the keyboard several times. Then he slams the lid shut, locks it and throws the key over the battlements like everything else.*

There is another candelabra with candles on the piano. The CAPTAIN *lights these. Then he goes to the whatnot on which there are several family photographs. He takes a photograph of Alice from its frame, tears up the photograph and scatters the pieces on the floor.*

The French doors blow in the wind and startle the CAPTAIN *again. He calms himself down. There are photographs of his son and his daughter in frames on the whatnot. He takes these photographs out of their frames, kisses them, then slides them inside his tunic near his heart.*

There still remain a couple of framed photographs of Alice. He sweeps these as well as the empty frames on to the floor, and then stamps on the lot.

After all his exertions the CAPTAIN *is tired. He slumps down at the writing table with the telegraph apparatus on it. His heart is hurting. He lights the writing candles and lets out a long drawn out sigh. He believes there's something moving around the room but he can't make it out. In the end he decides it's an hallucination.*

The CAPTAIN *lumbers back to the desk, lowers the flap and pulls out a bundle of letters tied with a blue ribbon. He hurries to the stove, opens the door, and throws the letters into the flames. He returns to the desk and closes the flap.*

Suddenly, the telegraph taps once and falls immediately silent. Very spooky, very startling. The CAPTAIN *looks around anxiously, his hand on his heart. He is listening for something, he is waiting for something. It is there, tantalizingly close, almost within earshot, almost within vision, but not quite.*

The CAPTAIN *stares at the telegraph, willing it to come to life. Silence. He goes across to the door leading to the kitchen and listens with his ear against the wood. Silence. He opens the door suddenly as if he expects to catch someone on the other side but there is no one there. He goes out and returns with a cat.*

The CAPTAIN *sits down and begins to stroke the cat. The gramophone finally stops. Silence. The* CAPTAIN *stands up and, with the cat thrown over his shoulder, goes through the door to the kitchen. Silence, then the sound of someone at the front door.*

Alice comes in from the porch. Her hair is pinned up again, the hairpiece is back in place and the grey hair is hidden. She is elegantly dressed in a walking coat, hat and gloves.

CONOR *appears on the battlements and sidles in through the French doors. He looks nervous.*

ALICE: It looks like Christmas.

CONOR: What's the form?

ALICE [*extends her hand for* CONOR *to kiss*]: You will thank me. [CONOR *kisses Alice's hand resentfully.*] My witnesses are irreproachable. The deposition is with the Colonel. He will contact us by telegraph, here in the heart of Balor's lair, shortly—

CONOR: I see.

ALICE: Not 'I see' ... I want to hear 'Thank you'.

CONOR: Why the candles?

ALICE: He's frightened of the dark, obviously. What does the telegraph remind you of? I think of it as grinder ... you put in meat, you get out worms.

CONOR [*noticing the photograph frames*]: What's he been up too?

ALICE: He's destroying all personal effects before prison ... the last desperate actions of a despot.

CONOR: Alice! That's horrible ... and unlucky. We were friends when I was young ... he helped me when I was in trouble ... I feel sorry for him in a funny sort of way.

ALICE: And what about me? I never harmed a soul *and* I sacrificed my career for this monster.

CONOR: Oh yes, your career. Weren't you famous ... in Ireland?—

ALICE : How dare you! Do you know who I am and what I was?

CONOR: Oh please ... don't roar like that—

ALICE [*looking tenderly at* CONOR]: You're tiring of me, already, aren't you?

CONOR: What?

[ALICE *throws her arms around his neck, and kisses him on the lips. In turn,* CONOR *bites* ALICE *savagely on the neck.* ALICE *screams.*]

ALICE: You bit me.

CONOR [*excitedly*]: Yes ... and I want to strip you, and then bite you under your arms, on your breasts, everywhere. When I arrived here on Crookedstone I was of sound character and proud of it. But the real me was imprisoned deep within ... and you set him free. Thanks to you I am filled with lust ... and I have so much power, I could throttle the life out of you with a kiss— [CONOR *embraces* ALICE.]

ALICE [*peeling off a glove and showing* CONOR *the ring finger of her left hand*]: See the mark of my ring? I was in bondage before ... but now I have no master.

CONOR: I'm asking ... let me be?—

ALICE: Yes?

CONOR: Your master.

ALICE: I thought you didn't like me.

CONOR: Wrong. The ferry hasn't left. We can be in an hotel in an hour ... then you'll see what I'm made of—

ALICE: And tonight you'll take me to the theatre. Everyone in town'll know then I've bolted and he'll be humiliated.

CONOR: Oh, prison isn't good enough then?

ALICE: No ... I want his face rubbed in the dirt.

CONOR: What a world. You abandon him but he gets the shame.

ALICE: That's the way the world is.

CONOR: These walls have soaked up the harm of every prisoner who passed through ... and now that harm seeps back into the air we breath. While you were contemplating the theatre, my thoughts were on my dear son.

ALICE [*striking him on the mouth with her glove*]: Idiot. [CONOR *lifts his hand to strike her back, then thinks better of it, and puts his hand down.*] Ah, your true colours.

CONOR: Forgive me.

ALICE: Kneel. [CONOR *goes down on his knees.*] Face to floor. [CONOR *lowers his face onto the carpet.*] Kiss my boot. [CONOR *kisses the end of Alice's boot.*] Don't ever do it again. Now up!

CONOR [*standing, puzzled*]: What's happening to me?

ALICE: You're in love.

CONOR: I am!

[*The* CAPTAIN *comes through the door from the kitchen, looking miserable and walking with a stick.*]

CAPTAIN [*breathlessly*]: I must speak to Conor, alone.

ALICE: What about?

CAPTAIN [*sitting at the sewing table*]: Conor, I only need a moment. [CONOR *sits grudgingly.*] Alice, could you please leave us in peace—

ALICE: Oh, a turnabout. Don't let me stop you, Conor! [*To the* CAPTAIN] Anything on the telegraph ... it'll be for me ... important! [ALICE *goes out by the door to the kitchen.*]

CAPTAIN [*after a long pause, speaking solemnly*]: Is there a purpose to a life like mine? Or ours?

CONOR: None.

CAPTAIN: So then what's the point?

CONOR: There isn't a point ... it's a mess, that's the point ... yet you've got to get down on your knees in front of it—

CAPTAIN: I can't bow before something with no fixed point.

CONOR: Look ... B is two miles south from C and eight north of D ... you can work out A! You're a mathematician.

CAPTAIN: I've looked ... but I never found it.

CONOR: Then your maths is wrong. Do the sums again.

CAPTAIN: All right ... but how can you be so forbearing?

CONOR: Come on ... I'm not always like this.

CAPTAIN: My guiding principle was always eliminate and move on. No one suffered on this earth the way I did when I was young ... so before I joined the army, I stuffed every childhood sorrow and adolescent defeat into a bag and I drowned the lot in the Irish sea. After that it was as if the pain had never happened.

CONOR: I am aware of that.

CAPTAIN: But what else could I do? I couldn't have gone on otherwise!

[*The* CAPTAIN *clutches his heart.*]

CONOR: Are you all right?

CAPTAIN: Terrible. [*Silence*] In every life there comes a moment when you know ... you're spent ... and then you see the future, and it's a horrible. [*In a thin, wavering, vaguely feminine old man's voice.*] My dear, Conor ... [*Normal voice*] I must apologise. What a show I've made of myself. In town, I saw Doctor Flood ... [*Reverting to the old voice*] He said ... it's hopeless ... my health's shot ... [*Normal voice*] He read the last rites!

CONOR: Did he?

CAPTAIN: I'm on my way out.

CONOR: So you lied.

CAPTAIN: Yes ... I won't live twenty years. [*Pause*]

CONOR: Were you lying about the other thing?

CAPTAIN: What?

CONOR: My son, who's ordered out here.

CAPTAIN: I don't know what you're saying .

CONOR: You're putting this on, aren't you?

CAPTAIN: Sorry, I don't understand—

CONOR: You're in bits!

CAPTAIN: Yes—

CONOR: Did you petition for a divorce?

CAPTAIN: Divorce? Who said anything about divorce?

CONOR [*rising*]: You're a liar, aren't you?

CAPTAIN: You're talking like a minister ... you sound ... intolerant.

CONOR: You want to forgive and forget, is that it?

CAPTAIN [*resolutely, in a strong voice*]: Yes, forgive me Conor ... for what I've done.

CONOR: Bravely put ... but there's nothing for me to forgive ... besides I'm not the man you think ... I wouldn't be worthy of your trust.

CAPTAIN: Life is full of such reverses. Childhood made me heartless and violent and I was happy to live like that but now I must give that up. [CONOR *walks over to the telegraph apparatus.*] What is it?

CONOR: Can you turn this thing off?

CAPTAIN: Only with difficulty.

CONOR: Who's Sergeant-Major Hibbert?

CAPTAIN: A wheeler-dealer but a good enough fellow.

CONOR: And the Quartermaster?

CAPTAIN: McBride, my enemy, but a good man in his way.

[*Footsteps and a moving lantern on the battlement*]

CONOR: Something's going on by the guns.

CAPTAIN: Can you see a light?

CONOR: Yes, and people moving.

CAPTAIN: That'll be a welcoming party.

CONOR: I don't follow

CAPTAIN: One of our little rituals. We always assemble by the guns before an arrest.

CONOR: Ah! [*Pause*]

CAPTAIN: Now you've got to know Alice again, how do you find her?

CONOR: I'm afraid, with people, the more I know, the less I understand. She's as much a mystery as you are ... or as I am. One of the few benefits of age is that I can now freely admit ... I know nothing. Yet I haven't stopped wanting to know. Why did you push her into the sea?

CAPTAIN: I don't know. It just seemed right. There she was on the jetty. Push her in! I thought.

CONOR: Did you regret it?

CAPTAIN: Never.

CONOR: How surprising.

CAPTAIN: What I really can't believe is that I did something so petty.

CONOR: Did you ever wonder if she'd strike back?

CAPTAIN: God yes, and she has, which is only natural.

CONOR: You spoke of my forbearance. You have it in buckets yourself. Where's yours from?

CAPTAIN: When you see death like I have ... you see everything anew. If you had to say who was right, my wife or I, who'd you choose?

CONOR: Neither. I'm sorry for you both ... well, with maybe a bit more on your side.

CAPTAIN: Conor, give me your hand.

CONOR [*shakes the* CAPTAIN *by the hand, his other hand on the old man's shoulder*]: My old friend.

[ALICE *enters, still in the coat, hat and gloves she wore earlier. In addition, she carries a parasol.*]

ALICE: God help us ... male friendship! Anything come in on the telegraph ... by any chance?

CONOR [*frostily*]: No.

ALICE: No more waiting. Conor, the time has come to finish him. One, load! ... if anyone knows the drill I do ... we have five thousand unsold copies of his manual in the scullery ... two, aim! three, fire! [ALICE *shoots with the parasol.*] How's the new wifey, Edgar? That young, pretty mysterious girl. Don't you know? There are no such mysteries with my lover. [ALICE *kisses* CONOR *passionately on the lips. It takes* CONOR *a moment or two to realise what is happening; then he pushes* ALICE *away.*] He's magnificent if a touch ... reticent. [*Stepping up to the* CAPTAIN] I never loved you ... and you're too vain to be jealous, and too vain to ever see that I have always led you by your nose.

[*The* CAPTAIN *draws his sword. He strikes at* ALICE *from his sitting position, but only manages to hit a piece of the furniture.*]

ALICE: Help! Help!

[CONOR *does not move.*]

CAPTAIN [*toppling to the floor, holding sword*]: Judith. Come here!

ALICE: He's down.

[CONOR *heads for the porch door.*]

CAPTAIN [*getting to his feet*]: But not yet out. [*Returning sword to scabbard then sitting at the sewing table*] Judith, Judith—

ALICE [*following after* CONOR]: I'm leaving. With you.

CONOR [*pushing* ALICE *back so she tumbles over*]: Away and back to hell. I never want to set eyes on you again.

CAPTAIN: Stay Conor. If you leave me she'll cut my throat.

ALICE: Don't walk out ... don't abandon us ... please!

CONOR: Go to hell! [*Leaves*]

ALICE [*in a different voice*]: Wretched man! Some friend!

CAPTAIN [*tenderly*]: Quick, tell me I'm forgiven.

ALICE: Conor's the most disgusting, two-faced so-and-so I've ever met. Thank God you're a man.

CAPTAIN: Alice ... quickly ... I'm going to die.

ALICE: Really?

CAPTAIN: The Doctor said.

ALICE: So the other thing was just talk too?

CAPTAIN: Yes.

ALICE: No divorce?

CAPTAIN: And no other woman! It was only ever you.

ALICE: What have I done!

CAPTAIN: There's nothing can't be fixed.

ALICE: Oh, yes, there is.

CAPTAIN: Rubbish. Just bury the past, drown it at sea, and push on.

ALICE: The telegraph. The telegraph.

CAPTAIN: What are you talking about?

ALICE [*kneeling at the feet of the* CAPTAIN]: I've destroyed myself ... done for us both! But how could you have let that man of straw in here to tempt me? We're finished yet we could have saved ourselves ... you could have forgiven me—

CAPTAIN: There's nothing that can't be forgiven. What haven't I forgiven you for?

ALICE: You won't get this in a bag and bury it at sea.

CAPTAIN: You're an evil schemer, I never doubted that, but I have no idea what you're saying—

ALICE: If I could undo what I've done ... I'd love you ... I'd take care of you, Edgar.

CAPTAIN: I wish you could hear yourself! Now come on, out with it!

ALICE: No one I can think of could help us ... no one mortal at any rate—

CAPTAIN: Can't somebody help?

ALICE [*looking* CAPTAIN *in the eyes*]: No. It's our children who've been destroyed. Who can help that?

CAPTAIN: What have you done ?

ALICE: Not I, alone, but ... they will leave school and go into the world, and they will hurt and harm others just as we have done. [*Pause*] You didn't really see Judith did you, when you were over?

CAPTAIN: No.

[*The telegraph comes to life.* ALICE *jumps up.*]

ALICE [*shrieking*]: Don't listen.

CAPTAIN [*calmly*]: What ever you say, dearest child ... just calm down—

ALICE [*listening to the telegraph while looking out the French doors*]: Don't listen—

CAPTAIN [*putting a finger into each ear*]: I'm not ... my ears are blocked.

ALICE [*listening to the telegraph*]: God help me! They're coming. They'll take him away ... and court martial him. [*Crying*] I'm an utter fool.

[ALICE *kneels and starts to pray. The telegraph goes on tapping and a long piece of paper curls out of the apparatus. Then, abruptly, the machine falls quiet.* ALICE *gets off her knees and goes to the telegraph machine. She tears off the paper and reads it. When she has finished reading she runs over to the* CAPTAIN *and kisses his forehead.*] Don't worry. False alarm.

[ALICE *throws herself into a chair and begins to cry. Beyond the French doors we see the lantern disappearing into darkness and hear the sound of men marching away.*]

CAPTAIN: What's that piece of paper, darling?

ALICE: Don't ask.

CAPTAIN: If you say so, my child.

ALICE: You wouldn't have said that before Conor came. What's happened to you?

CAPTAIN: I drew my sword ... I'm sorry ... then I fell ... I was dead for a second or so ... forget what I saw, exactly, yet it made a huge impression.

ALICE: Which was—

CAPTAIN: It made me hope ... for a better—

ALICE: What?

CAPTAIN: Life on earth ... because this is so unhappy, isn't it? It's like death, or worse.

ALICE: And us?

CAPTAIN: Well, we'll always torment each other!

ALICE: That seems to be our fate.

CAPTAIN: Yes, probably. [*Looking round the room*] We ought to get the place looking shipshape, oughtn't we?

ALICE [*getting up slowly*]: I suppose.

CAPTAIN [*standing and walking around the room*]: Or we can leave it.

ALICE: Yes, why not—

CAPTAIN: There's always another day! [*Pause. Sitting down again*]: It's a draw. I stopped you escaping ... you failed to kill me. Oh, and I know that you tried to have me arrested ... and you know, Hibbert and I, we didn't do anything. [ALICE *is astonished.*] But don't worry, that's buried at sea already. [ALICE *is silent.*] Anyway, its not the worst you've done—

ALICE: So now I have to be your nurse, is that it?

CAPTAIN: Would you?

ALICE: Do I have any choice?

CAPTAIN: It depends—

ALICE [*sitting, despairing*]: I can't believe this ... will it ever end?

CAPTAIN: You must be patient. Perhaps it's after death that life starts.

ALICE: If only! [*Pause*]

CAPTAIN: Is Conor a hypocrite or what?

ALICE: Absolutely.

CAPTAIN: Or maybe not ... we affect everyone in our orbit ... and the weaker they are ... like Conor ... the more powerfully our evil affects them. [*Pause*] Isn't modern life tedious? Once upon a time one fought, now you just sound off and make up later. No doubt Conor'll propose the toast at our silver wedding. Doctor Haverty will there, and his awful wife, and Hibbert, *and* McBride ... Colonel Beggs'll gate crash, naturally. Do you remember that wedding in Armagh, when Peter ... Peter Kelly got married to that girl ... she had to wear the ring on the right hand because he'd cut off the finger on her left in that fight they had! [*As* ALICE *laughs she holds her handkerchief over her mouth.*] Are you blubbing? ... ah no! laughter at last. One day we laugh, the next we cry, there's no logic to it. Is one better than the other? Who knows? The other day I read in the paper, a man married seven times, Frenchman of course, and at the age of ninety-eight, he re-married the first wife. Now there's love. Does life have meaning, or not? Haven't a notion. I only know that if you're too serious, Himself upstairs will trip you up and you'll fall flat on your face. That's what happened to Conor. Are you up for our silver wedding?

[ALICE *is silent.*]

CAPTAIN: The garrison will laugh at us ... what the hell. We'll laugh with them ... or maybe we won't. What ever! We'll please ourselves!

ALICE: Yes, why not!

[*The* CAPTAIN *takes the ring out of his pocket and slips it on Alice's finger.*]

CAPTAIN [*brightly*]: Our silver anniversary. [*Standing*] Drown the past and forge ahead. Come on, let's go to it!

Curtain

DANCE OF DEATH
Part Two

This version of *Dance of Death, Part Two* was first presented at the Tricycle Theatre London, Friday 27th March, 1998. The play was directed by Nicolas Kent. The designer was Monica Frawley. The cast was:

Captain Edgar Dawson	Michael Cochrane
Alice Dawson	Marion Bailey
Conor Coyne	Tim Woodward
Judith Dawson	Olivia Caffrey
Aidan Coyne	Luke de Lacey
Lieutenant Johnston	Richard Dempsey
Sentry	Dean Loxton

Edgar is in a Heavy Regiment of the Royal Artillery. The place is a British military facility on Crookedstone island off the north-west coast of County Donegal, north-west Ireland. It is Easter, 1916.

ACT ONE

SCENE 1

The interior of a Martello Tower converted to living quarters.

Beyond the French doors we can see long range guns lined along the battlement. The war is on and the canvas covers that protected the ends of the gun barrels in Part One *have gone. In the distance stretches the sea.*

This is the same room that we saw in Part One. *Two-and-a-half years on, it's a little shabbier, and there are also some additions—new framed photographs on top of the whatnot; an oil painting of Edgar in full ceremonial military dress; gas masks on the hooks by the porch door; and finally, on the writing table, beside the telegraph apparatus, a brand new 1915 telephone.*

Morning, Easter Friday. The French doors are closed. The SENTRY *is outside marching up and down.* EDGAR, ALICE *and* JUDITH *come in from the porch carrying hymnals.*

CAPTAIN [*tossing hymnal on chair*]: Bloody Easter Friday—

ALICE [*tidying hymnal away*]: That's crucifixion ... bloody business—

[*The* CAPTAIN *goes to his wardrobe and takes out a clothes brush.*]

CAPTAIN: Laugh! I thought I'd never stop. [JOHNSTON *enters with camera, tripod, plate box, flash pan and charger. The* CAPTAIN *brushes his jacket.*] Ah! Here at last. Put the camera over there, Lieutenant. [JOHNSTON *begins to set up the camera. Nearby, the Captain's daughter,* JUDITH *is clearing the table. She wears a short summer dress and her hair in a single plait. She looks fourteen but she is really eighteen or twenty.* JOHNSTON *can't keep his eyes off her. There is a knock at the front door. To* ALICE] Ah! that'll be your aloof cousin, Conor. Open the door. At last the Coyne clan are here. Conor, the Coyne who won't join.

[ALICE *opens the front door.* AIDAN *and* CONOR *stagger in with a chair like a throne, castors on the legs.*]

ALICE: You didn't carry that all the way from your cottage?

CONOR [*breathless*]: Yes!

CAPTAIN [*seeing chair*]: So you did bring it! Put it in front of the camera.

ALICE [*to the* CAPTAIN]: Do I hear a 'thank you'?

CAPTAIN [*brusquely*]: Thank you. If you fail the Woolwich exam, Aidan, you can always be a porter.

ALICE: Edgar!

CAPTAIN: And you too, dear Conor, should hard times come. [*Sitting in throne*] Yes. This is the job. [*Calling*] Johnston? How's this? Johnston!

ALICE [*to* CONOR]: He's quite disgusting this morning.

JUDITH [*to* ALICE]: No, he's not.

CAPTAIN: Good, stick up for me, daughter! Johnston, how do I look?

JOHNSTON [*emerging from under the viewing cloth*]: Fine, sir.

CAPTAIN [*tapping the arm rest*]: Judith ... here! ... and I want my student behind. [*Indicating to* AIDAN *where he is to stand*] Aidan, go on.

ALICE: And does your wife feature in this?

CAPTAIN: Course you do. Don't be so touchy! Where'd'you want to be?

ALICE: Usually the wife takes the chair and the husband stands, usually.

CAPTAIN: For an artist you're *so* conventional ... which luckily I'm not. Stand there ... let the world see the maturing actress still has her figure.

CONOR: Where shall I go? ... you've left me out—

CAPTAIN: Ha! in the cold ... well, you've only yourself to blame! Tell him where to go, Johnson.

JOHNSTON: Mr. Coyne, behind the chair, please, beside Mrs. Dawson—

CAPTAIN: But not too close to my wife, if you don't mind!

JOHNSTON: Thank you, everybody. [*All look forward. Johnston stands holding the pan aloft; lens cap off; a flash; smoke everywhere.*] One more. [*Cap back on; changes plate*] Cadet Coyne, please smile will you!

JUDITH: Yes, Aidan. You're always so glum.

ALICE [*to* AIDAN]: Don't listen to her.

[*Lens cap off; another flash; more smoke; cap on.*]

JOHNSTON: Done ... thank you.

[*The party breaks up.* ALICE *opens the French doors to let the smoke out.*]

CONOR [*coming up behind* ALICE]: The Captain's on form!

ALICE: Sizzling! He's got a bee in his bonnet about these shares.

[ALICE *goes through the French doors.* CONOR *and* AIDAN *follow.*]

JOHNSTON [*coming up to the* CAPTAIN]: I'd say that went pretty well.

CAPTAIN: Stop preening. [*Pointing to* JUDITH] Now, Johnston, I want one of just her.

[JOHNSTON *changes plate.* ALICE *slips back into the room. She watches what follows without the* CAPTAIN *realising.*]

JUDITH [*sitting in the throne*]: I'm dressed as a girl. Shouldn't I be wearing a longer skirt?

CAPTAIN: That's part of your charm, my dear.

JOHNSTON [*clapping hands*]: Oh, exquisite.

CAPTAIN: Don't be smutty! This is my daughter. [*To* JUDITH.] I want a smile. [JUDITH *beams.*] No, mysterious, enigmatic. [*After some thought.*] Like the Mona Lisa. [JUDITH *half-closes her mouth.*] Yes. [*Lens cap off; another flash; cap on.*]

CAPTAIN [*calling*]: Johnston! [JOHNSTON *comes over. To Johnston, confidentially*] Don't show that to my wife. Just pass it to me.

JUDITH: What are you whispering about?

CAPTAIN: Nothing!

[JOHNSTON *begins dismantling his equipment and putting it away. The* CAPTAIN *leads* JUDITH *away.*]

JUDITH: What's this, mother can't see my picture? [*Pointing at the whatnot where the other family photographs are arranged*] Isn't it for the gallery?—

CAPTAIN: Pipe down.

JUDITH: What are you plotting?

CAPTAIN: Nothing.

JUDITH: You are. You're smirking.

CAPTAIN: Am I?

JUDITH: Yes.

CAPTAIN: You truly understand me, don't you?

JUDITH: After eighteen years, I think I should.

CAPTAIN: Do you believe I have your best interests at heart?

JUDITH: Always.

CAPTAIN: Do you believe I would only do what's best for you?

JUDITH: Yes, but if it was good for you too, you'd like it even more.

CAPTAIN: How truly perceptive you are.

JUDITH [*curling two fingers together*]: We're a team, like that.

CAPTAIN: Yes, we are ... look, I tell you what ... I'd like you to do something ... make friends with the Colonel ... can you do that for me ?

JUDITH: Old Beggs!

CAPTAIN: Old! He's fifteen years younger than me, actually.

JUDITH [*amused*]: So. He's wrinkled, he's whiffy, he stares—

CAPTAIN: Do you want to stay on Crookedstone?

JUDITH: No—

CAPTAIN: Well then, we have to find you a way out, don't we? I've no money, do you understand—

JUDITH: But the Colonel ... he's—

CAPTAIN [*improvising*]: All right, he's old, but ... he's got qualities our young friends Aidan and the Lieutenant don't even know exist ... and he was a very good husband to his wife when she was alive—

JUDITH [*comically*]: Yes, which was about a hundred years ago!

CAPTAIN: Just have tea with him next week, that's all I'm asking ... and be nice to him.

JUDITH: And in return—

CAPTAIN: Oh, you want to bargain?

JUDITH: I'm free to talk to Aidan—

CAPTAIN: What! The boy's almost as boring as his father—

JUDITH: *And* the Lieutenant when and how I please, without you ticking me off—

CAPTAIN: Permission granted—

JUDITH: Plus—

CAPTAIN [*with pleasure*]: You are remarkable—

JUDITH: A copy of the photograph you're giving the Colonel—

CAPTAIN: Nothing gets past you, does it?

JUDITH: Why don't you like Aidan?

CAPTAIN: I do like Aidan.

JUDITH: You don't ... and the reason is ... you dislike his father.

CAPTAIN: You're wrong. It's not that I dislike either of them, it's that I understand the Coyne mentality, which is different. In life there are givers and takers. You are a giver, of course. Now Aidan and Conor, they're takers ... always got the hand out ... take, take, take, all the time ... . but then come the moment

you're short, oh no, they don't want to know you then ... anyway
... in a small garrison, if a man's selfish, like Conor, and won't
pull his weight, everyone finds out in the end ... they get their
come-uppance ... in his case richly deserved—

JUDITH: I'm sure Aidan'll pay you back ... one day.

CAPTAIN: Well, who knows—

[JUDITH *kisses the* CAPTAIN.]

ALICE [*calling out through the French doors*]: Aidan, where's your
father?

AIDAN [*coming in to room*]: He had to go.

ALICE: Well, if you see Conor, tell him I want a word.

CAPTAIN [*normal tone again*]: Alice, stop bossing. [*To* JOHNSTON *who
has just finished packing*] Johnston, take your camera, and go
away. Aidan, Easter it may be but we have work to do.

AIDAN: But my math's things are at home.

CAPTAIN: Well, go and get them then ... meantime, I'll see what I
can dream up to test that little brain.

SCENE 2

*The room in the Martello tower, later that same Friday morning. The
French doors are open.* AIDAN *sits at the desk, working on a fiendish
trigonometry problem. He uses compass, protractor and slide rule.*

JUDITH *appears outside the French doors. She creeps up behind the*
SENTRY *and prods him in the back with her tennis racket. For a moment the*
SENTRY *thinks a gun is being held to him. Then he turns and sees* JUDITH
with her racket. AIDAN *works on, oblivious of what is happening outside,*

JUDITH *creeps up to the French doors. She makes faces at* AIDAN. *Then
she takes off her straw hat and throws it. The hat lands on the desk.
Everything goes flying.*

JUDITH: Anyone for tennis?

AIDAN: I'm busy.

JUDITH: I've been waiting.

AIDAN: I'm busy.

JUDITH: But I left my bicycle *facing* the oak, not pointing *away*. You
must have seen it when you came back with your things.

AIDAN: So!

JUDITH: Well, what does it mean?

AIDAN: It means you want me to play.

JUDITH: No. It means, report to the tennis court, at once.

AIDAN: I can't. If I get this problem wrong, your father'll go berserk.

JUDITH: You really like the old monster ... or are you just pretending?

AIDAN: He's teaching me for free ... he takes a great interest in me—

JUDITH [*interrupting*]: Yes! you and the rest of the world. Come on!

AIDAN: I'd love to but ... I can't.

JUDITH: I'll get permission then. [*Shouting*] Daddy, I'm taking Aidan, he can't do your problem—

AIDAN: Judith!

JUDITH: Don't worry. He may not always know it, but father always wants what I want.

AIDAN: You're so hard.

JUDITH: Follow my example ... you might get your way for a change.

AIDAN: I'm not a wolf, like you, devouring everything.

JUDITH: So you must be a sheep ... Baa!

AIDAN: Yes, but a happy one.

JUDITH: Why won't you play tennis?

AIDAN: You know why.

JUDITH: Ah! it's the Lieutenant.

AIDAN: You only want me to play in order to hurt him ... well, I won't.

JUDITH: Am I that cruel? I never realised.

AIDAN: Well, now you know.

JUDITH: All right, I won't be cruel from now on, promise.

AIDAN: You can promise the world ... I won't believe you. You've got your claws into Johnston ... you don't need me. So go live your life somewhere else ... preferably a long way from me.

JUDITH: You really don't want anything to do with me, do you? [AIDAN *says nothing.*] Suit yourself, but we *are* going to bump into one another. [AIDAN *goes back to work.*] My father *is* preparing you for the Woolwich exam here in *my* house. [JUDITH *stands behind* AIDAN, *almost touching him.*] But have no fear, I'll try *my* hardest not to wolf you down. [AIDAN *can't stop himself looking round.*] Don't worry, the bad fairy will soon go. [*Pointing at desk*]

I just wanted to see a Dawson problem on the page. Thank you. [JUDITH *goes to the piano, lifts the lid, plays a chord, loud.*] I hear your father's had a Bechstein shipped across. Lucky you. [JUDITH *plays a second chord.*] We make do with this old thing. [*Closes lid*] Of course, if the war hadn't come and father gone back into uniform, we'd have only his measly service pension and we'd be even worse off. Yet even with his pay, we buy nothing, the place gets shabbier, I haven't had new clothes since I can't remember when. You are *so* lucky to be rich.

AIDAN [*politely*]: We're not rich.

JUDITH: You would say that, wouldn't you. Have I told you what lovely clothes you wear.

AIDAN: Yes.

JUDITH: How can you listen *and* do your sums? It's amazing.

AIDAN: You don't hear with your eyes.

JUDITH: Speaking of which, seen yours lately? Decidedly love-sick.

AIDAN: Go away.

JUDITH: Don't despise me!

AIDAN: I don't even think about you, so how could I despise you?

JUDITH [*reciting*]: 'Archimedes sat quietly at work,/When the Roman Centurion appeared.'

[JUDITH *ruffles Aidan's papers with her racket.*]

AIDAN: Leave them!

JUDITH [*triumphantly*]: Exactly! 'Leave my papers! cried the noble Greek,/And the soldier ran him through with his sword.' [*Normal voice*] I could live quite happily with you!

AIDAN: Leave me in peace.

JUDITH: Be nice ... I'll help you pass your exam.

AIDAN: You?

JUDITH: I know people.

AIDAN: Who?

JUDITH: People!

AIDAN: You mean your father and Lieutenant Johnston? They've no influence on anyone!

JUDITH: No ... but Colonel Beggs does.

AIDAN: Ah, I needn't work and you'll ensure the Colonel sees me right.

JUDITH: I resent your insinuation.

AIDAN: Cheating is wrong.

JUDITH: You're so vile ... sometimes—

AIDAN: And stupid for sitting and listening. Go away.

JUDITH: How can I go when I know you like me so very much!

AIDAN: Rubbish.

JUDITH: Always outside my window, aren't you? I take the ferry to Londonderry, you're always on it. You won't put the dingy out unless I help you unfurl the sail—

AIDAN: You're like a child, really.

JUDITH: Am I?

AIDAN: Delightful at times, but then you turn nasty.

JUDITH: Baa! said the sheep. Woof! I'll protect you said the wolf.

AIDAN: A wolf is a bad sheep dog.

JUDITH: Oh, very good!

[AIDAN *bolts for the French doors, but* JUDITH *gets there first.*]

AIDAN: I wish you were a man.

JUDITH: I thought you liked girls.

AIDAN: Get out of my way.

JUDITH: It's my house.

AIDAN: Move ... please.

JUDITH: What would you do if I were a man?

AIDAN: If you were decent you'd let me do my work.

JUDITH: What does that mean?

AIDAN: You don't get it, do you?

JUDITH: No.

AIDAN: A decent girl doesn't force herself on men, but an indecent girl—

JUDITH: You'll pay for that, I promise.

[JUDITH *backs out through the French doors, turns and speeds off.*]

AIDAN [*calling*]: Judith ... I'm sorry, I didn't—

[*But* JUDITH *has gone.* AIDAN *closes the French doors. He goes back to the desk, tries to work, fails. He begins to gather his things.*]

CONOR [*calling*]: Hello! Alice—[CONOR *comes in from the porch holding a bundle of letters. To* AIDAN] Oh, Aidan, hello. I forgot you were here.

AIDAN: Just finishing up.

CONOR: I hear Mrs Dawson was looking for me ... Was that her?

AIDAN: No, Judith.

CONOR: Ah, Miss Dawson. [*Putting letters down on the writing table*] How'd you describe Judith ... volatile ... decent?

AIDAN: No, thoughtless, selfish and devious.

CONOR: Such a harsh judge. And I thought you liked the family?

AIDAN: Captain Dawson's all right.

CONOR: He has his qualities. How about Lieutenant Johnston?

AIDAN: Inconsistent. And he's got a grudge against me.

CONOR: You're too concerned with the opinions of others. Forget them and just get on with your life. That's what I do.

AIDAN: Fine! but other people won't leave me alone. Once they bite, like that conger eel under the quay, they don't let go.

CONOR: You always see the worst and I thought you liked it here ... and don't you?—

AIDAN: I'm being smothered.

CONOR: Here, in the middle of the ocean? Surely you like the water?

AIDAN: Yes, open sea. But round here the water's clogged with jellyfish and eel and sea scorpions.

CONOR: You hatch indoors too much. Get out. Play tennis.

AIDAN: I don't want to.

CONOR: Judith's really the reason for this, isn't she?

AIDAN: Judith?

CONOR: If you carry on like this, you'll never have a life.

AIDAN: But I don't. I feel like the log at the bottom of the heap who'll never get to the fire

CONOR: Be patient. The pile will get smaller.

AIDAN: Yes, but meanwhile, I'm mouldering.

CONOR: It's terrible being young but have you any idea how we envy you?

AIDAN: All right! Let's swop places then.

CONOR: No, thank you!

AIDAN: You know the worst thing about being young? Older ones talking guff and having to keep quiet. You're not old by the way.

CONOR: You don't think so?

AIDAN: Not since I've got to know you, no.

CONOR: You didn't much like me after the separation, did you?

AIDAN: No.

CONOR: Did your mother ever show you a photograph of me?

AIDAN: One, very unflattering.

CONOR: I seemed old?

AIDAN: Yes.

CONOR: After I married, I went grey, overnight. That was the only photo Karen kept. Later, the colour came back but—[ALICE *appears at the French doors.*]—it's Alice! What do you think of her?

AIDAN: I'd rather not say.

CONOR: I won't ask then.

[ALICE *enters through the French doors carrying a parasol.*]

ALICE: Good morning, Conor, Aidan.

[ALICE *nods at* CONOR *indicating she wants to talk. To* AIDAN] Leave us. [AIDAN *begins to collect his things.*] Don't worry about those. Come back later. Go on.

[AIDAN *goes.* ALICE *sits on the chaise-longue,* CONOR *in an armchair.*]

CONOR: You were looking for me.

ALICE: This'll have to be quick. He went for the post. He'll be back soon.

CONOR: Perhaps I should go then ... so he won't find us alone?

ALICE: You're so moral, its nauseating.

CONOR: Only about myself. I don't tell others how to live.

ALICE: Aren't you just. I forgot myself once when I thought you'd save me and take me away. But you kept your head ... so we can forget what never happened.

CONOR: Fine, forget it.

ALICE: But he hasn't.

CONOR: You wonder why! You started his wake ... he wasn't even dead.

ALICE: Yes. Then he recovered, and for the last two years he's been waiting for the right moment to take revenge. Now I know the moment has come—

CONOR: You exaggerate. He's just a harmless old man.

ALICE: Beware his kindness. It's all put on.

CONOR: Yes, yes—

ALICE: He's creeping up like a big cat. I don't know why you won't listen.

CONOR: How come Aidan doesn't see this side? He's always with Edgar.

ALICE: He's a boy and obviously all *he* can see is Judith.

CONOR: Yes ... wouldn't it be funny if they ever got together?

ALICE: Would it?

CONOR: Oh yes.

ALICE: What do you actually know about Judith?

CONOR: She's a young girl in short skirts who likes to flirt.

ALICE: Yes. But wait till you see her in a long skirt, and with her hair up.

CONOR: She's old enough for that, all right.

ALICE: And she's old enough to play with Aidan.

CONOR: So long as it's just play.

ALICE: Oh, that makes it all right? [*Indicating throne*] When Edgar comes ... he'll sit there. You know you shouldn't have lent that. He'll steal it.

CONOR: He's welcome to it.

ALICE: Let him sit and talk ... you'll soon see how he plans to hurt you—

CONOR: You sound as though you know already—

ALICE: I don't. But I know the signs of a coming storm.

CONOR: You worry too much, Alice. I'm a good Quarantine Officer ... no enemies ... at least I think I don't ... what have I got to worry about?

[*Sound of someone at the front door*]

ALICE: He's spreading rumours ... you're not pulling your weight, financially—

CONOR: I've never seen you scared like this.

ALICE: Past courage you can put down to ignorance. Of the real dangers—

CONOR: Dangers ... I'm scared.

ALICE: If only. [*The* CAPTAIN *comes in with a bundle of letters, nods and sits in the throne chair.*] Let him speak first.

CAPTAIN: This chair you lent us, utterly superb, my dear Conor.

CONOR: Keep it. It's yours.

CAPTAIN: That wasn't what I meant—

CONOR: I did. After what you've given me ... it's the least I can do.

CAPTAIN [*garrulously*]: Nonsense. You know, when I sit here in my little fort, this Easter Friday, in the year of our Lord, 1916— [ALICE *sighs.*] Thank you, Alice. I remember Crookedstone was once called Hell's Island. Remember? But you, Conor, you've made yourself a Paradise in your cottage on the harbour. No Eve, naturally. Did you know the Prince Consort visited the garrison in eighteen ... [*He can't remember.*]—

CONOR: So I was told!

CAPTAIN: Speaking of princes—and since you live like one—don't you ever wish you didn't have me to thank for it?

ALICE [*to* CONOR]: Here he goes.

CONOR: Yes, I have much to thank you for.

CAPTAIN: Ah, stop it. Did you get the wine?

CONOR: Yes.

CAPTAIN: You liked it?

CONOR: Wonderful. Your shipper does you proud, tell him from me.

CAPTAIN: His stuff's first class.

ALICE [*to* CONOR]: So are his prices.

CAPTAIN: Did you say something Alice?

ALICE: No.

CAPTAIN: Well ... when the post of Quarantine Master came up, I thought of applying, meself. Made a bit of a study of the subject.

ALICE [*to* CONOR]: Liar.

CAPTAIN: I saw at once salt water was the way—

CONOR: Forgive me. I was for water. You were the oven man.

CAPTAIN: Rubbish.

ALICE [*loudly*]: No, Conor's right, I remember—

CAPTAIN [*interrupting*]: All right, maybe! Anyway, it doesn't matter because now we are faced—[*To* CONOR *who wants to interrupt*]—wait!—with a new situation. Quarantine is about to take a great leap forward—

CONOR: Speaking of which, did you read those stupid articles in the paper?

CAPTAIN: What of them?

ALICE [*to* CONOR]: Watch it. A 'scientist' wrote those.

CONOR [*to* ALICE]: Him! [*To the* CAPTAIN] What I meant was ... the writer wasn't fully informed, was he?

CAPTAIN: I wouldn't say that.

ALICE: Are you two trying to start a fight?

CONOR: No—

CAPTAIN: Everyone falls out here. We should set an example—

CONOR: Funny you say that ... when I went to get my letters just now, not one person said good morning. Have you had any unfriendliness?

CAPTAIN: I was at the post room just after you ... no, if anything, the reverse.

ALICE [*to* CONOR]: He's poisoned everyone against you—

CONOR: Not coming in on this new share issue couldn't be anything—

CAPTAIN: Oh no. But tell me, why won't you subscribe?

CONOR: Because all my money's already in the lime works. I have no more.

CAPTAIN [*pointing at an oil lamp*]: Proposition, my old lamp for this throne.

CONOR: All right.

ALICE: Watch it. He's feeling greedy.

CONOR: While we're on the shares ... I wouldn't want you to think my not coming in means I'm ungrateful or disloyal—

CAPTAIN: Well, it wasn't exactly loyal, turning your back on the business you helped to start and saying 'no' this time, was it?—

CONOR: I haven't got money to burn. I have to protect myself.

CAPTAIN: From what? Are you going to be robbed? Or bankrupted?

CONOR: Interesting words you choose.

CAPTAIN: Weren't you pleased when I got you six per cent?

CONOR: Course I was.

CAPTAIN: You don't sound it. But anyway, you're made as you are, you can't help it.

ALICE [*to* CONOR]: Listen to who's talking.

CONOR: No one is perfect, least of all me, but I never forget my friends.

CAPTAIN: Glad to hear it. [*The* CAPTAIN *reaches forward as if he intends to shake Conor's hand; but the action is a feint and at the last moment he bypasses Conor's outstretched hand, picks up a newspaper from the table, shakes it open.*] You'll never believe who's dead? The chief medical officer for the northern command. Oh, there'll be changes—

ALICE: Listen to him and the man's not even in the ground yet—

CONOR [*to the* CAPTAIN]: I never knew him ... what sort of changes?

CAPTAIN [*getting up*]: Well ... we'll find out.

ALICE: Where are you going?

CAPTAIN: Londonderry. [*Pointing at Aidan's things*] I hate the way the young think they have a right to clutter up one's house.

ALICE: He's coming back ... he'll clear it all away.

CAPTAIN: And where's he now?

ALICE: With our girl, I would imagine.

CAPTAIN: I don't like that. Judith'd better be on her guard ... and you, Conor, you'd better watch that young buck. [*The* CAPTAIN *lifts the lid of the piano and bangs out some chords.*] Dreadful tone. Not like your lovely German Steinbech, eh Conor?

CONOR: It's a Bechstein.

CAPTAIN: You've prospered, Conor. Be more grateful I got you here.

ALICE: No, he shouldn't! He got himself here.

[*The* CAPTAIN *looks up at the oil painting of himself.*]

CAPTAIN: The mess gave me that when I retired. Now there's real gratitude. By the way, you missed these at the post. [*The* CAPTAIN *picks a letter from his pile, examines the back, hands it on.*] Forgive me, I'm preoccupied.

CONOR: Of course.

CAPTAIN: And this one too. I was asked to hand it on, specially. [*The* CAPTAIN *stares at the stamp.*] Strabane postmark. I didn't know you knew anyone there.

CONOR [*taking the second envelope from the* CAPTAIN]: I don't.

CAPTAIN: Goodbye, you two. Must hurry ... ferry to catch. [*Leaves*]

ALICE: That first envelope he was looking at ... who's that from?

CONOR: It's something I've been keeping ... secret.

ALICE: Well, now he knows you might as well tell me.

CONOR: The Irish Parliamentary Party, Derry.

ALICE: So ... oh, I see ... you're standing?

CONOR: Yes, East Donegal.

ALICE: I bet he'll stand against you now ... as a Unionist.

CONOR: But he's never had political ambitions!

ALICE: Not until he saw you had.

CONOR: Is this why he's gone to town?

ALICE: No, that's to do with this Medical Officer dying.

CONOR: And what's that to him?

ALICE: You tell me. An old enemy perhaps and he's gone to gloat.

CONOR: He was bad enough in front of the camera earlier but just now—

ALICE: He was worse, wasn't he ... saying he got you the job, got you here, invested your money and that you're ungrateful. Lies. You got the job, you got yourself here and everyone gets six per cent! But he wants to eat you up, and one day, you'll wake up hollow like a rotten tree. You think you're friends but he loathes you—

CONOR: Hatred makes you perceptive, I see.

ALICE: And love makes you blind. Blind and thick.

CONOR: Stop it.

ALICE: Do you know what a vampire is? A dead soul inside the living. A parasite. Edgar's dead, has been for years. No interests or initiative or personality. But once he sinks his teeth into someone, gets his roots into their flesh, he starts to grow, and right now he's fixed on you. That's his nature. Plus he has a motive. You took me away—

CONOR: I didn't—

ALICE: Well, you nearly did! And now he has the opportunity ... the company's problems ... he can blame them on you—

CONOR: But it's fine ... and if he gets too close, I can shake him off.

ALICE: Like a leech? Just try.

CONOR: I can shake him off.

ALICE: He doesn't like Aidan either ... chasing Judith—

CONOR: He's not. If anyone's chasing anyone it's her—

ALICE: Think. It's a pattern. First you, now Aidan—

AIDAN: Nonsense—

ALICE: Yes ... and he wants to marry her off to his commanding officer—

CONOR [*shocked*]: Colonel Beggs, the widower? What does Judith think?

ALICE: If she could, she'd take the old Brigadier to annoy the forty-five year old Colonel. But then, given who her father is, are we surprised?

CONOR: Judith ... but she seems so nice and straightforward.

ALICE: Skin deep, I assure you. [ALICE *removes her gloves and sits down at the piano.*] Last time I failed when I tried to kill the monster but I have learnt from my mistakes.

CONOR: You have to load before you shoot.

ALICE: I know. With real bullets.

[CONOR *opens the second letter he got from the* CAPTAIN.]

CONOR: Maybe my being cut around the garrison is the least of my problems. Listen! [*Reading*]

There once was a traitor called Lundy,
Who fled from the city of Derry.
Now a chap called Coyne

Is doing the same,
And ditching ol' Donegal Lime.
Rem 1690. The Lime Boys.'
Oh God—

ALICE: Have you noticed how Edgar's changed since he went back into uniform? Now he's back in command, he's revitalised, eager to harm—

CONOR: Are you listening to me?

ALICE: Yes! You've had a letter from a crank.

CONOR: And now Edgar's gone to town and that always leads to trouble.

ALICE [*mock sympathetic*]: Ah!

CONOR: What's he going to do ... exactly? If only I knew. Perhaps ... you'll hear something ... and ... tell me?

ALICE: Providing there's no conflict with my interests ... my children.

CONOR: Of course. [*Pause*] It's so quiet suddenly.

ALICE: No, it isn't. Don't you hear it seeping from the walls ... mine and Edgar's arguments, our weeping and wailing, the gnashing of our teeth—

CONOR: Sh! I do hear something now. [*Pause*] No, it's only the gulls. I'll go then.

ALICE: I hear the voices, always.

[CONOR *leaves.* ALICE *sits at the piano, lost in thought.* AIDAN *and* JUDITH *appear outside the French doors. They laugh and then, suddenly,* JUDITH *casually slaps* AIDAN *twice and saunters off.* AIDAN *comes in. He doesn't notice* ALICE *at the piano.* AIDAN *is crying. He wipes his face with a small lace handkerchief and begins to gather up his things. Noticing him suddenly*] Aidan? [AIDAN *hides the handkerchief behind his back.* ALICE *is quiet, coaxing.*] What is it? I won't hurt you. Are you sick?

AIDAN: Yes.

ALICE: Come on ... what's really wrong?

AIDAN: Don't know.

ALICE: Headache?

AIDAN: No.

ALICE: In the chest is it?

AIDAN: Yes.

ALICE: Your heart's so sick, you think it'll split open.

AIDAN: How do you know?

ALICE: You want to die, you wish you were dead, and you can only think of one person. Someone else is thinking about her as well ... and that makes the pain much worse. [AIDAN *begins to pick at the handkerchief.*] It's a sickness that can't be cured. You don't want to eat or drink. You just want to weep in the cave under the cliffs, where none of the garrison will see you and laugh. Yet what do you really want? Nothing. You're too frightened to kiss her because you think then you'll die. And when you think about her, you think you are dying ... and you are. This is the death that gives life. But you can't understand any of this now. [ALICE *goes to* AIDAN *and takes the handkerchief.*] You think this is her? [ALICE *laughs.*] It is. She's everywhere, isn't she? Listen son, I know how much it hurts. [AIDAN *begins to cry.*] All right, have a good cry. [*Pause*] Now, that's enough, stop it! [ALICE *wipes his face.*] Otherwise the cruel one who isn't really cruel won't even look at you. [JOHNSTON *appears outside the French doors; he speaks to the* SENTRY; *only* ALICE *sees this. After a moment,* JOHNSTON *goes.*] I know she torments you, flirting with the Lieutenant. But take my advice. Make him your friend. Talk about her together. It'll help.

AIDAN: I hate the Lieutenant.

ALICE: Listen ... any day now Johnston's going to come looking for you because he's as unhappy as you. Haven't you noticed?

AIDAN [*happily*]: No.

ALICE: Yes. Judith hurts him, he needs someone to talk to. That should be you. Feeling better now?

AIDAN: Doesn't Judith want the Lieutenant?

ALICE: She doesn't want him or you. She wants the Colonel. [*Folding handkerchief*] I'm afraid I'm keeping this. Now go and get him.

AIDAN: The Colonel?

ALICE: No, the Lieutenant. He was out there just a moment ago. [ALICE *sits at the writing table and begins to write.* AIDAN *goes and opens the French doors.*]

AIDAN [*calling to* SENTRY]: Seen Johnston? Can you get him up? [JOHNSTON *appears at the French doors and follows* AIDAN *in.*]

JOHNSTON: Morning ma'am.

ALICE [*writing, not looking up*]: Sit down with Aidan. You're both unhappy for the same reason, so you can cheer each other up.

[JOHNSTON *and* AIDAN *sit on the chaise-longue.*]

JOHNSTON: It's terribly hot.

AIDAN: Yes.

JOHNSTON: Did you finish Book Six?

AIDAN: Nearly. I'm on the last problem.

JOHNSTON: It's a slippery one.

[*Silence*]

JOHNSTON: Did you play ... tennis today?

AIDAN: Too hot.

JOHNSTON: Tremendously hot, I agree.

[*Silence*]

JOHNSTON: Did you take the dingy out?

AIDAN: Couldn't get anyone to crew.

JOHNSTON: I will, if you'll have me.

AIDAN: Will you? That would be ... excellent.

JOHNSTON: I'm free at four.

AIDAN: Umh ... I'm hoping to give Judith a lesson then.

JOHNSTON: And I suppose you don't need another pair of hands?

[*Silence*]

ALICE: Who'll run me a message? [AIDAN *and* JOHNSTON *look at one another.*] To Judith? [AIDAN *and* JOHNSTON *both jump to their feet.*] Both of you. Well, we can be sure it'll get to her then. [ALICE, *reading the letter she has written*] 'Dear Judith, Here are your handkerchiefs which I have reclaimed from two foolish young men. I wonder if, in future, you could please desist from giving tokens as it only puts ideas into their silly heads. Your Mother.' [*To* JOHNSTON] The handkerchief, if you don't mind. Don't annoy me. She gave Aidan one, so she gave you one ... I know my daughter. [JOHNSTON *produces a second handkerchief. The two handkerchiefs and the letter go into an envelope which is sealed.*] She hates losing things and the Colonel doesn't want to play Othello. [*Handing envelope to* JOHNSTON] Give this to her, and keep your feelings to yourself. She hates lovesick men. [JOHNSTON *bows and leaves.* AIDAN *moves after him.* ALICE, *calling*]: Aidan!

AIDAN [*from the doorway*]: Yes?

ALICE: Did I say you could go?

AIDAN: But Johnston's going—

ALICE: Let him get hurt. You're going to take care.

AIDAN: But I don't want to take care.

ALICE: She'll make you cry.

AIDAN: Please.

ALICE: All right. But you're going to work ... you're going to Woolwich. Johnston can do what he wants ... and Judith ... is going away from here.

[AIDAN *runs out.* ALICE *goes to the piano and belts out a furious version of 'The Ride of the Whiteboys'. Curtain.*]

SCENE 3

The same, the following Monday. AIDAN *works at the desk on a problem.* JUDITH *is just outside the French doors fiddling with her bicycle.* JOHNSTON *sits a little way off.*

JUDITH [*coming in*]: Got a spanner?

AIDAN: Does it look like it?

JUDITH: You're just being rude now.

AIDAN: I'm not. I'm trying to work.

JUDITH: You're angry with me!

AIDAN: No!

JUDITH: I had to slap you on Friday ... you said I was indecent ... it was for your own good, you understand—

AIDAN: Was it? Well, thank you. Now I know you *can* be kind.

JUDITH: And having slapped you, I couldn't possibly have my sailing lesson at four, could I? [*Silence.* JUDITH *points at* JOHNSTON.] What were you and Johnston doing together all weekend? What were you talking about?—

AIDAN: None of your business—

JUDITH: Why are you so sharp?—

AIDAN [*standing*]: Right, that's it!—

JUDITH: Where are you going?

AIDAN: Out. If the Captain inquires, say his mad daughter drove me off.

JUDITH: Take the bike then.

AIDAN: What!

JUDITH: The pedal's loose, the seat moves and the handlebars wobble. Tell the Lieutenant. He'll fix it. He always does.

[AIDAN *goes out the French doors, takes Judith's bicycle and wheels it away.* JOHNSTON *gets up and goes off with* AIDAN.]

ALICE: That was quite a performance.

[ALICE *is standing inside the front door and has been for a while.*]

JUDITH: Oh, you. Where've you been? Having your walk ... in the prison yard, as you call it? In a real prison, those doors'd be locked, and the yard'd have a wall around it twenty foot high!

ALICE: Finished? Good ... can you listen for a moment?

[ALICE *sits on the sofa.* JUDITH *remains standing.*]

JUDITH: As long as you're quick. I hate long lectures.

ALICE: Don't you. It's time you put up your hair and wore a long skirt.

JUDITH: Why?

ALICE: Because you're not a child any longer. You must act your age.

JUDITH: What does that mean?

ALICE: You're old enough to marry ... grow up.

JUDITH: I see.

ALICE: Do you understand me?

JUDITH: Yes.

ALICE: In which case, will you please stop what you're doing to Aidan?

JUDITH: Are you serious?

ALICE: Yes.

JUDITH: Why should I stop! It's no skin off my nose.

[*While talking,* JUDITH *has lowered her cycling skirt and re-shaped her plait into a bun. Now she takes a hairpin from Alice's head and uses it to fasten her own hair in place.*]

ALICE: One doesn't normally perform one's toilette in the parlour.

JUDITH [*mimicking* ALICE]: 'We usually do this sort of thing in the bedroom.' [*Normal voice*] How do I look? Am I ready. Right then, come who dares.

ALICE: It's an improvement. Now will you please leave Aidan alone?

JUDITH: Why?

ALICE: He's suffering.

JUDITH: Oh yes, that's right. I did notice. But for the life of me I can't imagine why. I'm not.

ALICE: One day someone'll break your heart. Just be thankful, it hasn't happened yet. Now go and put on something long, something of mine.

JUDITH: And what are you doing now?

ALICE: What else is there to do on Easter Monday? We've prayed, we've exercised, that leaves only cards. Three way whist.

JUDITH: Do women walk differently to girls?

ALICE: Try.

JUDITH [*walking across the room*]: It's like my ankles are tied together.

ALICE: Once you gave up over socks for shoes. Now you must give up shoes for boots and a long skirt, and you must learn to walk very slowly towards the unknown, while all the time pretending you know exactly where you're going.

JUDITH: This is impossible.

ALICE: Oh, you'll manage it. You'll have to.

JUDITH [*kisses* ALICE *lightly on the forehead, then exits gravely like a dowager*]: Goodbye.

[ALICE *re-pins her hair, locates playing cards. A knock.*]

ALICE: It's open. [CONOR *comes in from the porch.*] Family don't have to knock. You know that—

CONOR: Is he here?

ALICE: Ah, you're being cautious. He was and he will be.

CONOR: What's the form?

ALICE: He's in the mess. Easter Monday, the officers come back to life by drinking sherry. It's a military tradition which lets him wear his medals.

CONOR: Which are?

ALICE: Every decoration you could mention.

CONOR: How many's that?

ALICE: Two. One that they gave him when he left ... which they had to.

CONOR: What's the other?

ALICE: Was it from the Portuguese? Yes. Arrived last month. Presented by the Colonel. I'm surprised he hasn't shown you, although now I think of it—

CONOR: Why did the Portuguese give him one?

ALICE: Didn't he write some articles about their quarantine conditions?

CONOR: That rings a bell.

ALICE: Not that he's been to Portugal or the Portuguese colonies, has he?

CONOR: I have.

ALICE: Exactly. When you arrived and had no friends and came here every night, why do you think he was asking all those questions? For his own amusement. Your stupidity then was amazing but the fact you still haven't understood is even more breathtaking. Anyway, it should be obvious to you now why he hasn't shown you that medal—

CONOR: Couldn't Judith have got him that decoration? She's thick with the Colonel, isn't she?

ALICE: Oh, really, there are limits and you've just over-stepped them.

CONOR: If we quarrel, we're finished.

ALICE: Keep your nose out of my affairs.

CONOR: Not where they touch mine, I won't.

[*The* CAPTAIN *appears outside the French doors.*]

ALICE: He's back.

CONOR: I wonder what will happen?

ALICE: We'll see.

CONOR: If he's anything to say, he'd better say it quickly. I can't stand the tension. Since I got that poison ... letter, no one's spoken to me except to answer my questions ... it's like being sent to Coventry—

ALICE: Yes, yes, now shut up. Sit on the chaise. He'll take the throne. I'll prompt.

CAPTAIN [*enters wearing full dress uniform, plus, on his breast, a long service medal and a Portuguese Order of Christ*]: Greetings.

ALICE: You look tired. Sit. [*The* CAPTAIN *flops unexpectedly on the chaise-longue beside* CONOR.] Are you all right?

CAPTAIN: Oh yes, very happy.

ALICE [*to* CONOR]: Be careful.

CAPTAIN [*crossly*]: What did you say?

ALICE [*to* CONOR]: He's had one too many.

CAPTAIN [*loudly*]: No, he has not. [*Silence*] Well, how have you two been amusing yourselves?

ALICE: Waiting. To play cards. With you.

CAPTAIN: Are you looking at my medals.

ALICE: No.

CAPTAIN: You're full of envy, aren't you.

ALICE: I've seen them before.

CAPTAIN: We get these things the way you actresses get laurel wreaths.

ALICE: I would never compare them.

CAPTAIN [*pointing at wreaths*]: Like those, that she got ... not from the audience mind [*to* CONOR, *confidentially*] but from the brother—

ALICE: Oh, be quiet, Conor knows perfectly well—

CAPTAIN: And in front of which I've had to genuflect every day for twenty-eight years. You know what a bully she is. She doesn't get her way, she denies you what only a wife can deny ... yet she isn't afraid to share it around with others ... is she? Oh no! [ALICE *looks at the ground.*] Well, Conor, lost your tongue?

CONOR: No.

CAPTAIN: Tetchy, are we?

CONOR: I'm waiting.

CAPTAIN: Ah, he wants news!

CONOR: Yes.

CAPTAIN: Has a little bird told you what he told me?

CONOR: You tell me.

ALICE: Yes, tell us.

CAPTAIN: Oh, ganging up, are we! [*Silence*] Cards you two? [*Silence*] But I came home specially to play. Don't disappoint me or I'll get cross.

[*They sit around the sewing table.* ALICE *deals. They start to play.*]

CONOR: How was your weekend across the water?

CAPTAIN: Thank you for asking. Alice, please note. Conor is making conversation. You should try it yourself. [*To* CONOR] It was very interesting and I come with news pertinent to your good self.

CONOR: Which is?

CAPTAIN: Oh, but I hate playing the messenger—

CONOR [*placatory*]: Go on.

CAPTAIN: Donegal Lime's going bust. A petition to wind-up the company'll be in the High Court tomorrow. Things have been rocky for months. Not enough houses being built apparently. Something to do with the war.

CONOR: Are you affected?

CAPTAIN: No. I sold my shares, well most, I maybe lost a few pennies.

CONOR: Lucky.

CAPTAIN: And yourself?

CONOR: You know as well as I do!

CAPTAIN: There's no need to be grumpy. I'm trying to be friendly.

CONOR: *All* my savings are in the company.

CAPTAIN: Well, that's your own fault. You should have either sold or subscribed to the new shares.

CONOR: Then I'd have lost all that too.

CAPTAIN: No, Donegal Lime would have stayed solvent then.

CONOR: You mean just the board. Surely the new issue was just a whip round for the directors.

CAPTAIN: What'll you do now?

CONOR: I'll lose everything, won't I?

CAPTAIN: How terrible. Mind you, that's what happens when amateurs speculate.

CONOR: When you first got me to subscribe, I was helping a local industry and creating a national asset. I was being patriotic. Now you call it speculation.

CAPTAIN: What do you plan to do now?

CONOR: Auction what I have, I suppose, get some capital quick.

[*The* CAPTAIN *plays the last card. Wins it. He has taken every trick in the hand.*]

CAPTAIN: I hope you'll do better than in cards. You'll need to.

CONOR: What does that mean?

CAPTAIN: The quarantine station's going to be moved onto the coast.

CONOR: I always said that's what we should do.

CAPTAIN: Did you? Really! Anyway, I saw the Colonel on Saturday. The subject of the old M.O. came up ... old fashioned man, resisted change ... anyway, I made some suggestions that went down rather well with Beggs. Apparently, they might even make me Q.M.

CONOR: I don't think so. I've a contract.

CAPTAIN: Yes, but they won't want a bankrupt in this garrison, will they?

CONOR: I'm not a bankrupt, yet.

CAPTAIN: But you will be.

CONOR: I'm going to sell what I have, get some cash. I'll get by ... I'll still have my salary.

CAPTAIN: I counsel discretion. No auction. You'll only draw attention to yourself.

CONOR: This is putting the cart before the horse. We don't even know for certain the company's bust.

CAPTAIN: I see scandal. You're a War Office employee who's speculated wildly in order to cause maximum embarrassment to his blood relations—

CONOR: If anyone's going to be embarrassed, surely that'll be me?

CAPTAIN: This could cost you your position, you know—

CONOR: Why will this affect my work? It hasn't anything to do with it—

CAPTAIN: But there've been complaints, dear Conor.

CONOR: About me? Rubbish.

CAPTAIN: Despite your many qualities, you're incompetent ... don't interrupt! ... the Colonel said so.

CONOR: This is news.

CAPTAIN: Either have the auction quick, somewhere far away, or find a private buyer.

CONOR: Sell, privately? Here?

CAPTAIN: You're not implying I want to sit in your chairs, or sleep in your bed, surely? That would be something. [*Begins to speak in bursts.*] Especially—if one remembers—as I do—what happened—the past—but not so far past it's forgotten—

CONOR: Not this, still. You mean what *didn't* happen—

CAPTAIN: What about your Aidan then?—and my Judith?—

CONOR: What about them? There's nothing happening.

CAPTAIN [*recovering*]: How's Alice? Become a turnip, have we?

ALICE: I'm thinking.

CAPTAIN [*recovered*]: Thinking is it! Well, if you must, make it sharp, accurate and correct, otherwise it's useless. Right you, think! One, two, three! Got there? No, you haven't. Right, I'll go. Where's Judith?

ALICE: Somewhere.

CAPTAIN: Where's Aidan? [*Pointing*] His things are cluttering up the place as usual. [ALICE *says nothing.*] Where's Johnston? [ALICE *still says nothing.*] Conor, tell me, what are you going to do with Aidan, now?

CONOR: Do?

CAPTAIN: Well, the Royal Military Academy at Woolwich is out. Even with a scholarship, your boy'd still need funds which you ain't got.

CONOR: I suppose.

CAPTAIN: What about the Indian army? They'll take anybody. Cheap too.

CONOR: The Indian Army!

CAPTAIN: Or put him to work. There's a war on, why not? He'd make a fine ledger clerk in a munitions factory. Now I know, Conor, you want Aidan to rise, socially, but maybe he'd be better off living among people of his own type. Frankly, I don't think he's capable of the standards of someone from my background—

CONOR: But you always said the British Army was blind to a man's religion—

CAPTAIN: Did I? I forget. How silent you are, Alice. [*The Morse code machine starts to click. Relieved*] Hello, what's this? [*Listening*] Oh, I don't believe it. Well, that's outrageous—

ALICE: What is it?

CAPTAIN: I thought you understood this thing!

ALICE: I wasn't paying attention.

CAPTAIN: That's your look-out then. Be quiet!

[*All listen as the machine clicks.*]

CAPTAIN [*darkly*]: I don't believe it—

CONOR: What?

ALICE: All army leave's cancelled—

CAPTAIN: I thought you weren't listening.

ALICE: I am now. All ranks are ordered back to barracks.

CAPTAIN [*to* ALICE]: Let me listen, will you!

ALICE: And all units are instructed to be in a state of military readiness. General mobilisation—

CONOR: Why? Invasion?

CAPTAIN: No. It's not an invasion, is it, Alice? Why don't you tell him? Wouldn't you enjoy telling him?

ALICE: No.

CAPTAIN: Oh, I thought you would.

ALICE: No, I wouldn't.

CAPTAIN: Go on, you would really. You love betrayal, you just love it, it always fills your heart with joy and your life with meaning.

ALICE: You tell him.

CAPTAIN: No, you tell him.

CONOR: Will someone tell me.

CAPTAIN: The message concerns a stabbing ... in the back—

CONOR: You'll have to explain.

CAPTAIN: From your lot—

CONOR: Don't follow.

CAPTAIN: I'm surprised a Home Ruler like you can't work it out.

ALICE: There's been a ... an insurrection of some sort ... in Dublin ... the post office and some other buildings have been overrun—

CONOR: By who?

CAPTAIN: I told you ... it's not the Kaiser ... . it's your lot ... who else? And if I may say so, how absolutely typical to do this on Easter Monday, while the boys here are were having a well deserved day off, and the rest of the army are up to their necks in Flanders mud. How very Irish—

CONOR: You won't provoke us.

CAPTAIN [*mimicking Conor's voice*]: 'Because we're as loyal as the rest of yous.' [*Normal voice*] Ha! The Roman Catholic always was a shabby, dissimulating, back-stabbing—

CONOR: Shut up. This has nothing to do with us. She's your wife for God's sake. And how long have *we* known each other? ... donkey's years. And have I ever shown any sign of disloyalty during that time? Never. And why would that be? Because I'm not disloyal. Yes, I believe Ireland should have her own Parliament, but within the Union, not outside it—

CAPTAIN: Please! No speeches. We're not on the hustings—

CONOR: I would never support violence against the state ... I'm employed by the state.

CAPTAIN: Did I say you did?

CONOR: Yes, you implied as much—

CAPTAIN: I didn't mean it.

CONOR: Why did you say it then?

CAPTAIN: It was quite wrong of me. It was the shock. Forgive me. I'm old. Come on you two, cheer up. This is a perfect example of fortune's wheel ... and like me you must learn to accept it. One moment, you're up top, cocky as can be, next moment you're on the bottom. We rule the country ... then we're knocked down. Temporary setback. But we'll be back up again. Et cetera. That's how it goes. Up, down, up, down. [*To* ALICE] Did you say something? [*She shakes her head.*] We've got an important guest coming next week, assuming this business doesn't interfere with his schedule. We must tidy the place up.

ALICE: Who?

CAPTAIN: The world might be on fire but you can always trust a woman to show interest if you say someone 'important' is coming. [*Standing*] I'm off to find my daughter. She'll want to know who's coming. [*Pause*] You know, perhaps it's for the best that you've no money and Aidan won't go to Woolwich now. Because of this nonsense in Dublin he'd have a rotten time with the English cadets, and you know what brutes the young can be. And I'm sure we can find something else for him ... get him off your hands, get him off the island. Is Judith playing tennis? [*Silence*] Don't all answer at once. [*Silence*] I see, I'll have to find her myself. [*The* CAPTAIN *goes out*]

CONOR: Who is this man?

ALICE: Don't ask me.

CONOR: How could he question my ... our loyalty?

ALICE: He just follows his nature. He thinks there's a weak spot, he goes for it.

[*Silence*]

CONOR: It must be the Colonel he's expecting.

ALICE: Must be. That's why he wants Aidan away.

CONOR: What do you think about that?

ALICE: I want Judith out of here by any means possible. If the Colonel's the route, so be it. At least Edgar and I agree about that.

CONOR [*standing*]: I'd better find my son then, hadn't I? See to his future.

ALICE: Goodbye.

CONOR: Goodbye.

[CONOR *leaves.* ALICE *goes to painting of herself, looks at it, shakes her head.*]

ACT TWO

SCENE 1

The same, a week later. It is raining outside and the Sentry's coat glistens with wet. The room is unchanged expect for a vase of flowers and new white antimacassars on the armchairs. ALICE *sits at the sewing table playing patience. The* CAPTAIN, *in his dress uniform, sits staring through the French doors at the rain outside.*

CAPTAIN: I love the rain.

ALICE: I don't. It's May Day. Where's the sunshine? It's not winter anymore, it's spring—

CAPTAIN: You have to love the rain to live here. Otherwise you go under. Alice, you know what your problem is?

ALICE: I don't but I know you're going to tell me.

CAPTAIN: You won't bend ... you don't understand that you must adapt to survive—

ALICE: If you say so—

CAPTAIN: And improvise continuously, although you'd call it plotting, which it isn't.

ALICE: I defer to your greater wisdom, dear, as always.

CAPTAIN: Where is that boy?

ALICE: Who?

CAPTAIN: Aidan?

ALICE: What are you improvising for him?

CAPTAIN: You're fishing.

ALICE: I'm asking.

[*A knock at the front door*]

CAPTAIN: Here he is. Ten minutes late. He won't survive the army if this is how he carries on.

ALICE: He's a boy.

CAPTAIN: Not with Judith he's not. He's a lecherous buck.

ALICE [*getting up*]: It takes one to know one, I suppose.

CAPTAIN: You do say the nicest things.

ALICE: You're putting him in the army, aren't you?

[*Another knock.* ALICE *goes out to the porch and opens the front door.* AIDAN *follows* ALICE *back into the room.*]

AIDAN: Captain Dawson, good morning.

CAPTAIN: You're late.

ALICE: Don't mind him. Give me that.

[ALICE *hangs up Aidan's dripping coat and returns to her cards.*]

CAPTAIN: Where's your father?

AIDAN: At the Quarantine Station. Four cases of scarlet fever came in this morning.

CAPTAIN [*calling to* ALICE]: Hey! You.

ALICE: What?

CAPTAIN: Get off your rump and go and get Conor up here.

AIDAN: I can run and get him.

CAPTAIN: No, she can. I want to talk to you.

ALICE: Why do you want to see Conor so urgently?

CAPTAIN: That's for me to know and you to find out. It's juicy, I promise. It'll be worth your while getting him. Go on. And the two of yous can run me down on the walk back. [*To* AIDAN] Alice loves to say terrible things about me to your father.

AIDAN: I don't think my father—

CAPTAIN [*interrupting*]: Joke! You'll never survive the army if you can't recognise one.

ALICE [*pulling on her coat, whispering*]: If I was to try and isolate one thing about you that I dislike more than any other, I couldn't. For the simple reason that I dislike everything about you.

[ALICE *hurries towards the porch.*]

CAPTAIN [*calling*]: So you don't like anything about me, at all?

ALICE [*from the porch*]: Always have to tell the world, don't you?

CAPTAIN: This is marriage, Aidan, be warned. [ALICE *goes out and slams the front door behind her.*] That was interesting. [*Silence*] When your parents separated, did you see a good deal of raw emotion?

AIDAN: No.

CAPTAIN: Kept it behind closed doors, did they?

AIDAN: Yes, sir.

CAPTAIN: Oh, please, call me Edgar.

AIDAN: Yes, Edgar.

CAPTAIN: Do you know what they're doing in Dublin today?

AIDAN: No.

CAPTAIN: The imbeciles who stormed the GPO surrendered Saturday. You know that?

AIDAN: Yes.

CAPTAIN: Now the clear up starts. And the courts martial. And there's only one way to punish treason. They should be shot, don't you agree?

AIDAN: Yes.

CAPTAIN: You agree?

AIDAN: Yes.

CAPTAIN: What does your father think?

AIDAN: The same.

CAPTAIN: Really. I thought he had a sneaking regard for the rebels.

AIDAN: No, sir ... I mean, Edgar.

CAPTAIN: You surprise me. Anyway, sit down.

[AIDAN *sits. A long silence.*]

AIDAN: You wanted to see me.

CAPTAIN: Yes. You know, I never tire of sitting here and looking out. Rain or shine, the ocean's always changing, always intriguing.

AIDAN [*turning and looking back over his shoulder*]: Yes.

CAPTAIN: Please don't agree with me just for the sake of it.

AIDAN: No.

CAPTAIN: I love the sea, especially when it rains. Now, tell me, the truth, do you?

AIDAN: Well, Edgar—

CAPTAIN: Go on.

AIDAN: It makes me feel hemmed in and breathless and sometimes I think I'm suffocating.

CAPTAIN: And are you?

AIDAN: Yes.

CAPTAIN: And you'd like to get out, wouldn't you?

AIDAN: Out?

CAPTAIN: Of the island. Because you feel trapped here. Isn't that what you just said?

AIDAN: Yes, only I couldn't right now because it'd hurt my father if I left.

CAPTAIN: Yes, I know. And I suppose Judith's an additional lure.

AIDAN: Judith?

CAPTAIN: Yes, Judith. My daughter. Remember. The girl you and that ridiculous Lieutenant chase after with your tongues hanging out.

AIDAN: We don't!

CAPTAIN: Oh, don't worry. I don't think you've done anything. But a father feels rather differently about a daughter than a son.

AIDAN: Yes.

CAPTAIN: How would you know? You don't have a daughter.

AIDAN: No.

CAPTAIN: Yet you agree with me as if you did?

AIDAN: I'm not.

CAPTAIN: Oh, you disagree. You want to argue with me then?

AIDAN: I don't, no—

CAPTAIN: I have higher things in mind for her than you. Understand? Nothing personal, you're very charming and sweet, but you couldn't support her. Not in her league.

AIDAN: No.

CAPTAIN: Oh, you think you are ?

AIDAN: Yes, no, no.

CAPTAIN: So you agree?

AIDAN: Yes, I'm definitely not in her league.

CAPTAIN: One day, when you have your own wife you'll see Judith as a milestone on your path through life, not a halting place.

AIDAN: Yes.

CAPTAIN: Isn't it nice when two gentlemen agree?

AIDAN: Yes.

CAPTAIN: Shall we see if we can keep this up?

AIDAN: I hope so.

CAPTAIN: Did you know you're leaving us.

AIDAN: I can't.

CAPTAIN: Oh, but you can, you will, and besides, you said you wanted to.

AIDAN: I can't leave father now.

CAPTAIN: Yes, your father. He is a rather unfortunate man. [*Silence*] Parents seldom understand what's best for their children ... that is ... of course there are exceptions. Hm! Tell me, Aidan, are you in regular contact with your mother?

AIDAN: Of course, she writes.

CAPTAIN: You know she's your legal guardian?

AIDAN: Yes.

CAPTAIN: Did you know she's given me power of attorney, over you?

AIDAN: No.

CAPTAIN: You do now. Your travel papers are at the main guardroom with Corporal James. Take the next transport across, and then the train to Dublin. You're to report at the Royal Barracks tomorrow, from where you'll be shipped on to Salisbury for basic training. What's the matter?

AIDAN: Do I have to go right now?

CAPTAIN: What did I just say?

AIDAN: What about my father?

CAPTAIN: He and I have agreed, you should go quietly, no emotional farewells. So get your bags packed, and get yourself to Dublin. You're to report no later than six hundred hours. You haven't long. Get moving.

AIDAN: What about money?

CAPTAIN: It's taken care off.

AIDAN: Then I have only to thank you.

CAPTAIN: I like gratitude. I wish others were the same. Hm! [*Raising voice*] You know the Colonel?

AIDAN: Not personally.

CAPTAIN [*underlining his words*]: He's a personal friend [*Speeding up*] and he has chosen to take a close interest ... in my family and my wife's also. [*Speaking with increasing difficulty*] He has succeeded in obtaining money ... for you. I hope ... you and your father ... understand the debt you owe him. [*Indicating desk where* AIDAN *works*] Take your things, go, you'll get money with the travel papers. Now ... I must lie down—

AIDAN: Are you ill? Shall I get the doctor?

CAPTAIN: I'm never ill.

[*The* CAPTAIN *goes to the internal door, disappears.* AIDAN *begins to pack up his papers, pencils, books. A knock at the French door. He turns and sees a strange woman in a cape with a hood. She carries an umbrella. The figure enters. It is* JUDITH.]

JUDITH: Aidan?

AIDAN [*looking at her intently*]: Is that Judith?

[JUDITH *wears a long dress and her hair is pinned up.*]

JUDITH: It's me! What is it? The long skirt? My hair? You haven't see me like this before?

AIDAN: No.

JUDITH: I've been in Londonderry ... shopping. On the way back everyone on the ferry was talking about the surrender in Dublin but I paid no attention. I had all my old school clothes packed and ready in a bag filled with stones. As we reached the deepest point between the mainland and here, I threw it in the sea and watched them sink. I look like a woman now, don't I? [AIDAN *turns away.* JUDITH *speaks earnestly.*] What are you doing?

AIDAN: I'm going.

JUDITH: Where? What about your exam? It's not for months.

AIDAN: I have to report to barracks in Dublin tomorrow.

JUDITH: When do you leave?

AIDAN: Now.

JUDITH: Whose idea was this?

AIDAN: Your father's.

JUDITH: Obviously. [*Walks a few paces, stamps her foot.*] I wish you could stay. The Colonel's coming. You should meet him. Good contact.

AIDAN: You wish I could stay because the Colonel's coming?

JUDITH: Yes. Must you go?

AIDAN: I have to, and *now* I want to.

[*Silence*]

JUDITH: This island's a prison, isn't it? and the inmates are all speculators. In lime and human beings. [*Silence*] Once I was blind and I was happy. Now I see and it hurts.

AIDAN: You?

JUDITH: Yes.

AIDAN: Are you all right?

JUDITH: I'm choking.

AIDAN: Are you?

JUDITH [*as if in pain*]: Ah! This is how it feels. You poor boy.

AIDAN: If I was cruel like you, I'd laugh now.

JUDITH: I wasn't cruel before, just ignorant. You can't go.

AIDAN: I must.

JUDITH: Give me something first.

AIDAN: What?

JUDITH: I can't let this happen. Let's sail off together in your dingy ... and we'll sink her out in the sound, together, far away from the eels and the jellyfish. Yes? But we should have washed the sails ... I want them pure white ... the last thing I want to see is pure white ... then you'll swim with me in your arms until you tire and then we'll sink. That's far more beautiful than grieving for each other and scribbling secret letters that father is going to open and read. Are you listening?

AIDAN: Why didn't you say any of this before?

JUDITH: I didn't have the words.

AIDAN: And now I have to leave ... but I suppose it's for the best. I couldn't compete with a Colonel—

JUDITH: Don't mind him.

AIDAN: But it's true!

JUDITH: It is and it isn't.

AIDAN: Could it become untrue?

JUDITH: Yes.

AIDAN: Is that a promise?

JUDITH: How long until I see you?

AIDAN: I don't know. A year.

JUDITH [*jubilantly*]: A year. I could wait a thousand but then if you don't come, I'll spin the earth backwards, the sun will rise in the west, we shall travel back to this moment and that next time I shan't let you go. Hold me. [*They embrace.*] Don't kiss me. [*Turns away her head*] Now, go! [AIDAN *gathers his belongings, pulls on his coat, embraces* JUDITH, *goes out, comes back.*]

AIDAN: I can't do it. When you're kind, it's another Judith who appears ... and that one's mine. She won't fail me, will she?

JUDITH: No. I won't. [*The sound of coughing and retching*] What's that?

AIDAN: Oh ... your father ... he went upstairs, he's not ... well—

JUDITH: Let him come. Nothing frightens me anymore. Take me under your coat. [JUDITH *wraps Aidan's greatcoat around herself.*] I could run away with you to England. You'll join a regiment. The ones in the bearskin hats. Handsome uniform, suit you well. [JUDITH *fondles his hair.* AIDAN *kisses her finger-tips, then kneels and kisses her feet through her boots.*] Are you mad? Stop that! You'll get black on your face. [*He rises.*] Then I won't be able to kiss you. Take me with you.

AIDAN: On basic training? I couldn't.

JUDITH: Could.

AIDAN: I'd be arrested.

JUDITH: Me too.

AIDAN: I must get ready, there isn't even time to say goodbye to my father.

JUDITH: I'll swim after the ferry. You'll have to jump overboard and save me. It'll be in the papers. We'll get engaged.

AIDAN: You can't ever stop joking, can you?

JUDITH: Anyone can weep, but to laugh, that's an exception.

[AIDAN *and* JUDITH *embrace passionately.* AIDAN *goes out the French doors and into the rain.* JUDITH *follows after him and they embrace again outside.*]

AIDAN: Go in. You'll get soaked.

JUDITH: What do I care. [AIDAN *disappears.* JUDITH *comes back in. She takes a cigarette from a box on the writing table. She lights it. She inhales, coughs. She picks up the telephone. Pretending to speak on the phone.*] Could I speak to the Colonel, please? Is that Colonel Beggs. Hello. This is Miss Judith Dawson. I'm afraid there's been a misunderstanding. I am in love with Aidan Coyne, a far better man than you could ever be. And how dare you imagine that my young body will ever warm your tired old body in your stale dirty bed.

[JUDITH *laughs and laughs. Blackout.*]

SCENE 2

The same. Thirty minutes later. It is still raining. One of the French doors is open and bangs in the wind. JOHNSTON *appears at the French doors, knocks, waits. No answer. He comes in and closes the door behind.*

JOHNSTON: Lieutenant Johnston here. Hello? Captain Dawson? Telegram. [*Silence. Calling*] Hello? Anyone home? Telegram, from the Colonel, just arrived. [*He props the telegram against the telephone, goes to leave, thinks better of what he has done.*] No. Everything in its place and a place for everything as Captain Dawson would say. [*He picks up the telegram and goes through to the porch. Calling from the hall*] I've left the telegram in the porch. On the letter tray. I'm going now. Goodbye.

[*The sound of the front door slamming. Rain and wind. Voices.* ALICE *and* CONOR *appear outside the French doors and enter.*]

ALICE: Have you really no idea why he wants to see you?

CONOR: None.

ALICE [*sniffing*]: Can you smell tobacco? I thought he'd given up.
[ALICE *finds the remains of Judith's cigarette near the telephone.*]

CONOR [*sitting*]: Is it today the Colonel's coming?

ALICE: Yes, this afternoon I think. Now where is he?

CONOR: The place looks different.

ALICE [*bad English accent*]: 'One must look one's best when the Colonel comes, what what.' [*Calling, normal voice*] Edgar, I've got Conor. [*To* CONOR, *brightly*] I know what I meant to ask ... are you still going forward as a candidate?

CONOR: No news to the contrary. I expect to hear any day now.

ALICE: It's time some good came your way. Imagine if you got elected.

CONOR: With everything going to be sold, the cottage lost, and a move into barracks imminent, yes, it would be ... something.
[*A muffled noise from above.*]

ALICE: He's upstairs. [*Calling*] Edgar! Conor's here, come down.
[*The* CAPTAIN *comes through the door from the kitchen. His uniform is creased, his hair stands on end; he looks deathly.*]

CAPTAIN: Forgive me—had to lie down—not feeling myself—

CONOR [*rising*]: Are you ill?

CAPTAIN: No, I'm not. I don't get ill.
[*The* CAPTAIN *sits heavily in the throne chair.*]

CONOR: Alice said you wanted to see me.

CAPTAIN [*amiable but vain*]: Yes, I have information to impart. Sit.

CONOR: I'm all ears.

CAPTAIN: Well. [*Pompously*] The subject of quarantine has been neglected in this kingdom for the best part of a century. However, quarantine was never more desperately needed than now, in the midst of this great war that is raging both abroad and latterly, at home as well—

ALICE [*to* CONOR]: He's been practicing—

CAPTAIN: Happily, thanks to unprecedented developments now taking place—

ALICE [*to* CONOR]: Communications, of course—

CAPTAIN: On every front, the Government has decided to encourage further research and for this purpose have created a Quarantine

Inspector.

ALICE [*to* CONOR]: What?

CAPTAIN: Me!

[*Silence*]

CONOR: Congratulations.

CAPTAIN: I will be, in effect, your superior, but this will not affect the ties of blood that bind us. Now, to turn to other matters. I have arranged for Aidan to start his basic training.

CONOR: He's not ready.

CAPTAIN: I'm afraid your wishes take second place to those of his mother. Your wife having granted me the authority to decide the boy's future, I have decided. He's in the army now.

CONOR: I admire you.

CAPTAIN: That all you can say? Don't you have any human feelings on being parted from your son?

CONOR: I should be suffering, should I?

CAPTAIN: Yes.

CONOR: You'd be glad to see me suffer?

CAPTAIN: But can you suffer, Conor? When I was near to death, and you were present, all I can recall was your unalloyed joy at the thought of what was almost within your grasp ... Alice, my wife—

ALICE: Not true. He sat up all night with you. He stopped you going mad, since when you've shown not an ounce of gratitude—

CAPTAIN [*pretending not to hear her*]: Aidan has to leave us. He'll be gone by this afternoon.

CONOR: But I haven't even a penny to give him.

CAPTAIN: Money, money, always money. I ... or actually ... we ... a consortium interested in his future—

CONOR: A consortium!

CAPTAIN: Yes ... where's the list?

[*The* CAPTAIN *searches in his pockets and finds the sheaf of papers. He hands these to* CONOR *who reads them.*]

CONOR: These are all charities.

CAPTAIN: Whatever.

CONOR: Have you been begging for my son?

CAPTAIN: Ungrateful as always. Ungrateful friends are the worst!

CONOR: I'll be called a pauper, living off British Army charity. That's my candidature finished—

CAPTAIN: What? For Westminster. Haven't you understood anything? The army rooted out the rebels but then victory wasn't their aim ... martyrdom's what they want, and by God, they'll be getting it. They'll be shot, rightly, and then the Irish, that's your lot, Conor, and her people, but not my people, will be appalled, and they'll swing behind Sinn Féin ... don't shake your head, I'm right. And then your Irish Parliamentary Party ... they'll be on the dunghill, Conor, and you along with them. Oh, it's goodbye Redmond ... cheerio democracy and Home Rule step by careful step ... hello, Pearse and Connolly, they're the future now. Parliamentary candidate for East Donegal! Ha! You'll lose your bloody deposit.

[*Silence*]

CAPTAIN: You don't seem bothered.

CONOR: You've taken everything else! ... yet you want more?

CAPTAIN: But have you more? Do you wish to reproach me? Think first—have you any grounds on which to reproach me?

[*Silence*]

CONOR: Strictly speaking, none! Everything is above board ... on the surface—

CAPTAIN: On the surface ... you're so cynical, but then that's your nature. You know at moments like these, I'm tempted to agree with Alice's long held opinion. At bottom, you're a fake and a hypocrite.

CONOR [*calmly*]: Is that Alice's opinion?

ALICE [*to* CONOR]: It was, once ... but I was wrong, totally wrong—

CAPTAIN: All right ... I can be generous too. Conor, go and say goodbye to Aidan. The ferry leaves at three. Go on.

CONOR [*standing*]: This isn't so bad. I still have a job. I've known worse.

CAPTAIN: As you've often said. Makes me wonder about America. What did you get up to?

CONOR: Nothing. I just met misfortune. It's the right of every human being to meet misfortune.

CAPTAIN [*sharply*]: Did you bring these misfortunes on yourself?

CONOR: They were matters of conscience.

CAPTAIN [*curtly*]: You have a conscience?

CONOR: The world is divided between wolves and sheep. It's no honour to be a sheep, but who'd be a wolf?

CAPTAIN: I prefer what they say in Belfast. 'Each man creates his own luck anew each morning.'

CONOR: Oh, is that a saying?

CAPTAIN: A man's strength as you should know—

CONOR: Oh, I learnt what I know about strength when yours failed on that couch—

CAPTAIN [*raising voice*]: Look at me! I fought for fifty years alone agin the world and I won because of steadfastness, devotion to duty, energy, and my sense of honour! And I never chased a skirt!

ALICE: Let others be the judge of that!

CAPTAIN: But will anyone admit this publicly? No ... because everyone's jealous of me, aren't they? However ... honour comes to he who waits ... a visitor is expected ... today, Judith is going to meet her future. Where is she?

ALICE: Out, I think.

CAPTAIN: In the rain? Fetch her.

CONOR [*standing*]: I think I'll go.

CAPTAIN: No, wait. Is Judith properly dressed?

ALICE: I presume. Did the Colonel definitely say he was coming today?

CAPTAIN: Yes, but he should have sent a telegram with his arrival time. Have any telegrams come?

ALICE: How would I know?

CAPTAIN [*rising and shuffling towards the porch*]: Then I'll have to check, myself.

[*The* CAPTAIN *goes out.*]

ALICE: Is this a man?

CONOR [*sitting down*]: Before I always said no, but yes, he is. He's the most typical man I've ever met. And aren't we the same? Don't we also use people, and exploit opportunities? That's all he does.

ALICE: He's eaten you and Aidan ... how could you defend him?

CONOR: I've met worse. And I still have my soul. He couldn't eat that.

ALICE: What 'worse' have you known?

CONOR: You should know?

ALICE: Are you trying to be offensive?

CONOR: Of course I'm not. So, don't ask.

[*Outside it stops raining. The* CAPTAIN *comes in from the hall holding a telegram in his hand.*]

CAPTAIN: It was on the letter tray the whole time. [*Handing the telegram to his wife and sitting down in the throne chair*] I've lost my glasses. Read, Alice. Conor can stay. [ALICE *tears open the telegram, reads the message, then looks up, astounded. She smirks then quickly wipes the look off her face.*] Well! Are you worried? [ALICE *looks at her husband without speaking. The* CAPTAIN *continues caustically.*] Who is it from?

ALICE: Colonel Beggs.

CAPTAIN [*beaming*]: Thought so. What does it say?

ALICE [*reading*]: 'In view of Miss Judith's insolent and disgusting telephone message, our relationship is terminated.'

CAPTAIN: Sorry, once again.

ALICE [*reading loudly*]: 'In view of Miss Judith's insolent and disgusting telephone message, our relationship is terminated.' [ALICE *looks at the* CAPTAIN.]

CAPTAIN [*bleakly*]: Judith!

ALICE: So you must be her Holofernes.

CAPTAIN: You did this?

ALICE: I didn't.

CAPTAIN [*incandescent with rage*]: You did this!

ALICE: No, not me, this is all Judith!

[*The* CAPTAIN *rises and tries to draw his sword. He gets the blade halfway from the scabbard and then collapses with a stroke.*]

CAPTAIN [*tearfully*]: Don't be angry, I'm old, I'm ill.

ALICE: Are you? I'm glad, because you deserve to be.

CONOR: We should carry him to his bed.

ALICE: I don't want to touch him.

CAPTAIN: Alice ... Conor ... don't be angry. [*To* CONOR] Think of my children.

CONOR: Oh, choice. Feel sorry for his children and he after sending my son away—

ALICE: How can he be so blind?

CAPTAIN: I did it all for my children.

[*The* CAPTAIN *begins to blub and ramble unintelligibly.*]

ALICE: At last! Your tongue's stopped and your lying, bragging, wounding days are done. Conor, you believe, don't you? Well, please, thank Him above. He has freed me from prison and ground my jailer under His heel.

CONOR: Stop it, Alice!

ALICE [*putting her face against the Captain's*]: Where is your 'strength' and your 'energy' now? [*The* CAPTAIN *spits in her face.*] Still spitting? I'll have your tongue out. No! [ALICE *strikes him across the face.*] I'll cut off the snake's head. Ah Judith, you have freed us. Have you more heads? I'll cut 'em all off. [*Twisting the Captain's ears*] Conor, you must ask Him to forgive me. [*The* CAPTAIN *is in real pain.*] Before I never believed in His justice but now I do and now I'll be one of His lambs, like you. Tell Him Conor ... Non-stop torment makes us wolves, but one smile from Him and we believe.

[JOHNSTON *appears at the French doors with a letter. He knocks and comes in. He doesn't see the* CAPTAIN *in the throne chair.*]

JOHNSTON: I'm terribly sorry to barge in. I left a telegram and I wanted—

ALICE [*releasing the* CAPTAIN]: Yes, we got it.

JOHNSTON: And I met Miss Judith on the quayside ... she was seeing off the transport ... [*waving letter*] ... and she wanted me to bring Captain Dawson this letter—

ALICE: Not now. Help us, please.

JOHNSTON [*seeing the* CAPTAIN]: Is he all right?

ALICE: No. Very bad, I should think.

JOHNSTON: I'll get Doctor Haverty.

ALICE: Too late.

JOHNSTON: Oh.

ALICE: Wheel him out. He can look his last on the sea. Go on. Do it.

[JOHNSTON *turns the throne chair round and wheels the* CAPTAIN *through the French doors, stopping just beyond them.*]

ALICE [*opening other doors, flooding room with light*]: Open all the doors. Let in the air.

JOHNSTON [*loudly*]: Captain Dawson, sir, your daughter gave me a letter for you. Sir, can you hear me? [*Coming back into the room*] I have this really urgent letter. What should I do?

ALICE: Later.

[ALICE *gives* JOHNSTON *a blanket and pillows and propels him away. Outside,* JOHNSTON *makes the* CAPTAIN *comfortable.*]

CONOR: You're abandoning him?

ALICE: The ship is sinking. The crew must save themselves. The gulls can have his eyes. His body will do for fertilizer. 'Once the spark's out, you're a barrowful of garden muck.' Isn't that what he always said? Myself, I will go to my room, strip naked and wash every crevice where his filth has stuck to me ... if I can.

JOHNSTON [*coming back in*]: I'm terribly sorry and I know this isn't the time but ... Miss Judith was desperate that the Captain read this—

ALICE: Oh give it to me then—

JOHNSTON: But, Miss Judith was insistent the Captain read this. It's a private letter—

ALICE: Hand it over. [*Takes letter.*] Outside. [JOHNSTON *goes.* ALICE *opens the letter.*]

CONOR: My son has gone and I never said goodbye.

ALICE [*reading letter*]: Ha! [*Turning to French doors and raising voice*] Listen Edgar. [*Reading from letter*] 'Father, you're not small minded, you hate sentimentality and you're a real aristocrat. You won't want me around after the telephone call I made. You shouldn't have tried to saddle me with the old man Beggs. I've gone with Aidan. I love him. Goodbye. Judith.'
[*The* CAPTAIN *slumps; blanket and pillows spill to the ground.* JOHNSTON *picks them up.* ALICE *hands* CONOR *the letter.*]

ALICE: Flowers blossom in filth. [*While* CONOR *looks at Judith's letter,* JOHNSTON *comes back into the room and coughs.*] Yes?

JOHNSTON [*pointing at the* CAPTAIN]: I'm afraid it's over.

ALICE: Oh, God [*checking herself, turning to* JOHNSTON] thank you.
[CONOR *goes out. He puts Judith's letter in the Captain's hand.*]

ALICE [*to* JOHNSTON]: Did he say anything before he died?

JOHNSTON: Yes.

ALICE: What?

JOHNSTON: 'Forgive them, for they know not what they do.'

ALICE: Extraordinary.

JOHNSTON: He was a loyal and decent man.

ALICE [*calling*]: Conor, come here.
[CONOR *comes back in through the French doors.*]

ALICE: His last words ... 'Forgive them, they know not what they do.'

CONOR: Meaning?

ALICE: He was always right and the world was always wrong.

CONOR: Well, there'll be fine words at his funeral all right.

ALICE: And wreaths from his Lieutenants.

CONOR: Certainly ... and the Colonel.

ALICE: But now he's dead I don't want to speak ill of him.

CONOR: Why would you?

JOHNSTON: He was a loyal and decent man, Captain Dawson.

ALICE [*to* CONOR]: Hear that! [*To* JOHNSTON] Go to the Captain, go on.

[JOHNSTON *goes outside and stands awkwardly near the body.*]

CONOR: 'They know not what they do.' When I asked you in the past you always said he didn't know what he was doing. He saw opportunities. He took them. If that's right, then you must forgive him.

ALICE: At last there is peace here. The quiet that comes from death ... it's as marvellous as the noise of birth. I hear the silence, can you? ... I see the lines on the floor made by the castors when he was wheeled away. My fate will be his ... but my life is not over ... yet. The Lieutenant was right. Edgar was loyal and decent ... my husband, love of my youth ... he had his qualities, his virtues—

CONOR: He was brave and not afraid ... to fight for himself.

ALICE: He went through every misery and humiliation but he blotted them out and got on with living.

CONOR: Except he ... did he know how to live ... did he know how?

ALICE: As you were talking ... I saw him as he was when he was young ... I must have loved that man.

CONOR: And hated him.

ALICE: Yes ... *and* I hated him ... but I hope he knows peace, now, while I begin to live ... at last ... like a woman. Hold me. Hard. [CONOR *wraps* ALICE *in his arms.*] Harder.

[*They do not move.*]

Curtain

Letters to Nicolas Kent

LETTER 1

18th April, 1997

Dear Nicolas,

After I spoke to you on the phone, I took the momentous step of making a file called *Dance of Death, Part One* and I actually started on the new version of *Part One*. I've made some progress over the last couple of days, and now (at this moment of writing) I am several pages into it.

Here are some of the things that I have in mind:

My plan is to make the Captain, an Ulsterman (and Protestant) and Alice (a Dubliner and Catholic); their daughter Judith (as would have been the convention at the time), will therefore have been brought up in her Mother's faith. (Kurt, when I get to him will also be RC: I will rename him Conor.).

At the moment Alice is an aspiring Catholic, who speaks with a received ('Donnybrook') Dublin accent (which has been achieved with the help of elocution lessons). However, when her husband annoys her, or gets under her skin, then her accent slips, and she becomes more 'Dublin' (but never stage Oirish). And when the accent slips, it may well be that the Captain will then 'take her off' with uncanny and very hurtful accuracy.

The setting, at the moment, is a Martello tower crammed with furniture collected over many years of garrison life.

I'm also thinking that the characters are much older than I realised when we spoke. I think the Captain is in his late fifties, early sixties, while his wife a sprightly late forties. (Perfect parts, therefore, for Michael Gambon and Prunella Scales.)

Some general thoughts on the plays and their qualities and themes:

1) Both plays have a berserk, lurching quality (which I hope very much to retain). The more I read *Part One* (and *Part Two*) the more it strikes me that the characters are spiralling out of control. Both plays strike me as the very anti-thesis of the 'well-made' play.

Both plays, but *Part One* particularly, have fantastic energy and wonderful moments of truthfulness (although *Part Two* does have a few of these it must also be admitted).

Michael Meyer (the best-known British translator) believes this quicksilver quality is one of the reasons for the enduring appeal of the *Dance of Death* and I think he's right.

2) When I took *Part Two* to pieces (as I did to prepare the précis), I discovered what a ramshackle thing it is; some of it doesn't make sense, it contradicts itself in places, and there are an awful lot of duff scenes in

which exposition is established and plot advanced in an incredibly lumpy, unsophisticated way that is the antithesis of good theatre.

More than anything, *Part Two* strikes me as being like a rather disreputable person who succeeds *entirely* due to the sheer force of his personality. Frankly, it's amazing the thing stands up at all given that the narrative is so poor and the theatrical situations are so threadbare. The problem that faces me, after *Part One*, is how will I make of this a compelling narrative?

3) The answer lies (to some extent) with realising what the plays are; they are an account of a marriage and that marriage, like a dance at a ball, has been contracted into and that contract can never be broken. The two parties, Edgar and Alice, must move together, as one, until death kills one or the other off. They cannot live without each other, yet they cannot prevent themselves, when they are together, so huge is their hatred, from trying to kill each other. However, because they also provide the other with a reason for living, (as well as a reason for hating), when they lash out at each other, they always end up hurting themselves as well.

4) The clearest revelation of Strindberg's message seems to come at the end of *Part Two*. Having spent four hours hating her husband, Alice does a volte-face the second he dies and starts praising him.

When I first read this, I thought it was completely preposterous, but the more I think about it, the more I believe there's a great deal of truth in it. Literary history is littered with these kinds of U-turns; Hardy's attitude to his first wife after her death being the example that springs to my mind.

But there is more, in Strindberg's end, than simply the truth that spouses will love in death the partner they hated in life. It is also part of Strindberg's design that Alice praise her husband, despite everything that has happened, at the end of part *Part Two*, and the reason Strindberg has her do this is because she did love him; and therefore, she does wish him well, she does wish him peace. He has sustained her; not just in the distant past (when they were happy) but right up to the moment of his death.

However, blinded in life by her hatred, it is only in death that she sees and recognises the simultaneous presence of both benign and antagonistic forces in her life.

At least, I think that is Strindberg's philosophy (and how very Ying and Yang it seems when so expressed). I am absolutely certain that one of the ways in which the new *Part Two* can be made to seem to arise naturally out of *Part One*, is by having Strindberg's credo inscribed in the text. (Yuk, what a sentence).

4) Now, I am a long way from the end of *Part Two*; I am at the start of *Part One*, but Strindberg's message (which is clearest at the end) has been

stamped into every crevice of the play, and if *Part One* is to succeed, this quality must be absolutely manifest in my re-translation.

5) The other reason for going on about the Strindberg zeitgeist, is because of how it connects to his enduring appeal.

I would not say what I am about to say in public because it is deeply un p.c., but it seems to me that Strindberg understood something about male/female relationships which the Feminist theoreticians of the late twentieth century would have us believe is a lie.

The contemporary line, as I understand the theoreticians, is that 'gender relations' are all about power. Putting it a different way, modern Feminism has imposed a class template on men and women and so they see gender conflict in the way the Marxists saw class conflict (and look where that got us).

However, our subversive friend from Sweden sees marriage as a state of mutual interdependency, no different from all sorts of other interdependencies which underpin life in the natural world. He believes marriage relations are simultaneously nourishing and parasitic; they feed and destroy; they are benign and destructive; but they cannot be done away with because in the ecology of the psyche (as in the natural world) everything is interdependent and no one part can opt out. (I think that sentence could go into Pseud's Corner in *Private Eye*).

The Captain and Alice have a relationship like animals in the natural world; they support one another but at the same time they are competing with one another. They are endlessly trying to do each other down; but they also do love each other. In the words of the old song, they can't live with one another, or without one another.

And the more I read these plays, the more I see that this is the truth that they speak, for all their darkness.

6) I offer these thoughts to give an indication of how I see the plays— or how I'm beginning to see them. I also want to say that I feel enormous sympathy for them. In fact, I have to confess, that as I started work on *Part One*, reading my Meyer and other translators, then closing the book and re-imagining and reinventing of the dialogue I had just read in an Irish idiom, I felt the most tremendous surge of excitement. This felt so right. Will this last? you may wonder. We shall see. I think it will. I have a very good feeling about this project.

Now, to another matter, and then I shall terminate this letter. Do you remember the postcard which I sent with the précis of *Part Two*? it showed a man in a street in the former Yugoslavia. The photographer is David Barker. It was his company, DBA, that I used to work for in Belfast. David is principally a film cameraman; he shot and produced that film about the three wives and the gun I made that you liked. Anyhow, he's shut DBA; he's still working as a film cameraman but he wants to branch out as a stills photographer. He's been taking stills for years; he has a huge archive; and now he wants to exhibit some of them. Do you think it would be at all profitable for him to speak to you about possibly hanging his pictures in your restaurant exhibition area? He's got some sensational photographs of prisoners in the Maze, and at the moment he's working with the last Women's Accordion Band on the Shankill. He's also got lots of other photographs from Jamaica, South Africa, America, and so on. If you wanted to contact him, his details are at the bottom of that card.

Finally, do you have any translations other than the Meyer? Also, the Frank McGuinness 'Vanya' is awfully good.

Well, I'm going to sign off now.

I hope you're well. Warmest wishes from here

Carlo

LETTER 2

13th June, 1997

Dear Nicolas,

Here it is—and what a huge, huge pleasure this has been. It is not too Oirish—which I didn't think you wanted—but I hope it's sufficiently Hibernicised for your tastes. More Green can be added if required.

You should know that I have used three translations in the preparation of this version. They are:

a) Strindberg, *Plays: Two* translated by Michael Meyer, Methuen, 1982.

b) *Dramas of Testimony: The Plays of August Strindberg*, translated by Walter Johnson, University of Washington Press, 1975.

c) *Eight Best Plays* by August Strindberg, translated by Edwin Björkman and N. Erichsen, first published as *Ten Famous Plays* (1950) and reissued 1979 by Duckworth, London.

I don't think you'll find any line in mine in any of the above. What I did when 'writing' was to read a page, close the texts, and then write from memory in my own words, and then check what I'd written against the above to ensure there was no unconscious plagiarism. It was a very interesting exercise. To begin with I found it incredibly hard work; it was exhausting and I made little progress; however, once I got the voices of Edgar and Alice and Conor in my head, I was off, I was unstoppable.

One of the keys to my discovering the 'voices' was my realisation that in my version, humour must loom large. Incidentally, I don't think this is a betrayal of Strindberg; I suspect that in the original Swedish the play could be hilarious too. When I was writing, I kept imagining a Hibernicised John Cleese as Edgar, a Hibernicised Prunella Scales as Alice, and a Hibernicised Richard Briers as Conor. I'm not certain any of these actors could do this (I'm not seriously proposing them) but I say this really as a shorthand way of describing the mood that informed me and the way I think the piece could be put over. I sincerely believe this could be funny and tragic at the same time. It also seems that humour might be a way of getting an audience.

And now some points in no particular order:

1) Names. Edgar and Alice are very good Irish names and translate directly. Although Kurt is not unknown in Ireland it's not an immediately Irish name. He is Conor.

2) The laurel wreaths. According to my inquiries, laurel wreaths are a sign of academic distinction in Scandinavia. The implication, therefore, in the original play, is that Alice is a university graduate although Edgar thinks the wreaths were awarded to Alice for her acting. (In other words, Edgar's misunderstanding would presumably be found funny in Scandinavia—but not here it won't.)

Taking a leaf from Strindberg, I did toy with the idea of Alice being a university graduate but I rejected this on the grounds that it would unduly complicate the back story. However, I have added some props which indicate that Alice has achieved some academic distinction.

As for the laurel wreaths, in this version they are now what Edgar always thought—something to do with Alice's stage career. I also toyed with the idea that Alice is shown wearing one of the wreaths in the oil painting of her in costume that hangs on the wall but bottled out because I thought this was a bit too knowing. What do you think?

3) Music. 'The Ride of the Whiteboys' is a made up title; no such pieces exist. However, I shall speak to some 'musical experts' at some point soon and see if I can't identify some real piece that would do the trick. 'The Ride of the Whiteboys' must be a really evil sounding reel or jig. Of course you might want something specially composed but I'll ask my contacts anyway.

4) Old Woman. Her last line, before she leaves Edgar, could be in Irish. What do you think?

5) Back story. On the whole, I believe, my 'new version' is a faithful rendering in new language of the original. The only real change I've made (and it's one of emphasis rather than invention) concerns Conor and Alice. I've pointed up their adolescent relationship and underlined their attraction. When Alice thinks (at the end) that Conor is going to take her away, she sincerely believes that she is going to become his lover. He also believes this.

A fully paid up Freudian might also posit that the reason Conor comes to the island in the first place is in order to steal Alice and he almost succeeds; in other words, Conor is not the goody-two-shoes that he is described as being in all the critical essays on the play that I have read. I found this idea attractive but decided, in the end, not to point it up in my version; the Freudian interpretation of Conor as wife stealer seems to me to be a decision that should be made by the director (you) and the actor rather than me—and with the text that you have here you can either play Conor as a wife stealer, or as Strindberg's Christian alter ego (which is what most critics describe him as).

I think this letter has gone on quite long enough.

I hope you like the enclosed.

My oh my, I have so enjoyed doing this.

Warmest wishes

Carlo

LETTER 3

6th August, 1997

Dear Nicolas,

First of all, I got the Swedish text of the *Dance of Death*. A brilliant idea of yours and my goodness what a revelation it is. Strindberg's text is quick and airy and impressionistic, whilst the translations (even the Meyer, which is excellent), are heavy and long and wordy. The easiest way to express what I mean would be with a musical comparison; if Strindberg's text were a score it would be a jig or a reel, full of tiny quick notes that speed along, while the translations, if they were a score, would be something by Strauss, stately, portly, full of gravitas, but without any air or lightness or speed.

The other really telling and interesting thing about the Swedish original is the way that the text *isn't* run continuously (as in the translations); no, every time a character goes off and a new one comes on, the text is divided with a slash; the text stops. During my struggles with *Part Two* (when I say 'struggles' what I mean is that I've been thinking about it a lot) I've been troubled by the way the play (as it stands) has characters endlessly shuffling on and off the stage in a way that seems somewhat forced. But now I see how Strindberg wrote the piece; he wrote it with breaks between the scenes; and suddenly I see that he never intended either *Part One* or *Part Two* to be played as a continuous block but had a much more what we would call 'cinematic' style in mind; what he obviously intended is that the play not be played as an unbroken piece but would be played as a series of episodes with breaks—blackouts, musical stings, pauses, what ever—between the segments, even though the material forms a seamless chronological whole. In film terms these breaks would be effected by fade outs and indeed Bergman (greatly influenced by Strindberg) does exactly the same thing in his films (like 'Scenes from a Marriage'). Bergman has long blocks of chronlogically coherent material which he carves into shape with fades. Anyway, this is an incredibly long winded way of arriving at an incredibly simple point; when I go back to *Part One* and when I write *Part Two*, I'm going to put these breaks in (as slashes—like in the Swedish text) and I think they will change the way the text reads. They will break it; they will also act as time lapses.

When I got your text, I then decided as an experiment that what I would do was to sit down (I did this yesterday—I only got back on Saturday) with it, the Swedish text, and my published translations and re-translate the first two scenes in *Part Two*; I decided I wanted to jump into *Part Two* rather than go back to *Part One* because a) I need to hear Judith and Aidan's voices and b) by translating a bit of *Part Two* I thought that I could shoehorn myself into thinking more coherently about the overall structure of *Part Two*. Anyway, I sat down, with the Swedish and the published English translations and set about work, and, well, it was an extraordinarily interesting experience doing this and having the Swedish text to hand. Because I saw how quickly the Swedish text whizzes along, I made myself write English that went just as quick. And as I did this, I saw, suddenly all sorts of things (as you predicted would happen when I saw the Swedish). I saw that what I've done with *Part One* is to produce something faithful in sense but lacking Strindbergian airiness. I also saw that the way to sort out *One* is to cut it, to cut it a lot—maybe by as much as a third. I also saw that one of the very simplest but most efficient ways to work is to look at the Swedish, read it, see how it inflects, count the number of words in the sentence and then make the English work that way, and never to let the English have more words than the Swedish. To do this is, surprisingly, far easier than it sounds.

Another thing I saw is that by keeping the text simple and quick like the Swedish, although every nuance and meaning isn't down in black and white on the page, somehow the meaning is there and more emphatically so than in the more loyal and detailed that is my version *Part One* as it stands at the moment. This really is a case where less actually is more. This discovery reminded me of an observation Hemingway made; he said that what one cuts or leaves out of a text nonetheless remains as a ghostly presence within the text; even though one takes the words away, nonetheless the meaning remains, just as something in a painting that's been painted over nonetheless continues to shine through; and furthermore, said Hemingway, the reader picks up the meaning even though the text is cut. This sounds a bit arty but I do believe it's true.

Another interesting thing that I saw when translating the first few pages of *Part Two*, was that Meyer's version of *Part Two* is markedly, noticeably less good than his translation of *Part One*. His *Part One* is quicker and more 'Strindbergian' than his *Part Two*. Now *Part Two* has problems in terms of its stage craft but buried in the text (and not revealed by Meyer), and this I discovered as I translated, is a powerful, desperately painful psychologically authentic story about children and parents and how children both absorb and reject the predelictions of their elders. It was extremely interesting to discover that there was this heart of Strindbergian pain that is every bit as potent and dramatic as the pain in *Part One* beating inside *Part Two*.

Another discovery that I made translating the first few pages of *Part Two* is how much the play is a continuation of *Part One*. *Part One* is about a couple locked in a terrible dance of death—they can't live with each other, they can't live without each other, and they want to kill each other—and in *Part Two*, I discovered, that is also the story, except that in *Part Two*, not only do we have our core dysfunctional couple, Edgar and Alice, we also have the children, Judith and Aidan. And in simple terms, that is what I propose my version of *Part Two* be about—the relationship between the generations.

I said above that the children both replicate and reject the defining qualities of their parents and I want to talk about that for a moment. Judith, it seems to me, is a fantastic character, on the brink of adulthood and torn between turning into the psychic vampire that is her father, or turning into a rather reasonable, loving, well adjusted, unselfish woman. Aidan is Conor; decent, honourable, but pliable and weak as well. (He's less interesting than Judith.) He is in lust with Judith and, which is so typical of men of his age, he hides his feelings behind a front which is curt and dismissive. However, what complicates things further is that his instinct tells him that Judith is dangerous; she could go the way of her father; he knows this with his head; Aidan, in his heart, however, still yearns for Judith.

The dynamic that develops, or the story that I want to tell in my version (taken from Strindberg) goes something like this. Judith wants Aidan but can't decide whether to achieve her goal by using her father's methods (flirting with other men and making Aidan jealous) or through the honest revelation of her own feelings. In the end, she goes for the latter (and incidentally destroys her father by dumping the Colonel), but of course her emotional openess involves her in feeling pain. At the moment she declares to Aidan that she wants him, she loses him (literally—he's sent off to the war—or will be in my version). This in its turn connects to her father and the theme which runs through *Part One* and will run through *Part Two*; Edgar's system of living is essentially a way of avoiding his feelings; he blots out, he scrubs out, he throws into the bottom of the sea everything he hates about his life and his childhood and his own behaviour; by this means he is able to continue, untroubled by conscience or guilt; however, this mode of existence also guarantees that he doesn't have any of these, not in the way we understand them; all he has is a Nietschean will to triumph and control. I'm making a terrible meal of this but what I'm trying to say is that the Judith story in *Part Two* is the story of a girl torn between two ways of living and in the end she goes for the way that isn't her father's way and this is certainly one of the contributing causes of Edgar's death at the end.

Now Edgar's story, I think, must be the continuation of what was established in *Part One*. He's now retired; he doesn't have any money; the living room looks shabbier than in *Part One*; he can't even afford to mend a broken pane of glass in the French door; however, in contrast, the guns on the battlements outside are bigger and more powerful than in *Part One*. The War Office is in the middle of a war; it can spend; but no cash is flowing Edgar's way. Edgar is also (continuing from *Part One*) still harbouring a grudge against Alice and Conor because for a moment they were about to run away together and desert him. He wants to get even and his story in *Part Two* is how he sets about trying to do this. I think we should retain the idea that Edgar inveigles Conor to put money into a company which he knows will fail and then enjoys the spectacle of that company failing. I think we should also keep the idea that Conor is expecting and hoping to stand as a Parliamentry candidate—in this case for the Irish Parliamentry party (Redmond's lot—the anti-Sinner Nationalist, pro-Home Rule crowd). For Conor to stand for this party and for his son to go in the army would be historically accurate: Redmond actually asked Irishmen to serve in the British Army in France at a speech at Woodenbridge, Co. Wicklow, in 1914; and in return, said Redmond, the Government of Ireland Act (shelved in 1914) would be immediately enacted after the war. I don't think we can retain the Strindbergian conceit that Edgar decides to put himself forward for election in the same party when he discovers that Conor is standing; I think it very unlikely that a Protestant like Edgar would stand for the Irish Parliamentry Party; he's much more likely to stand as a Unionist; so to keep this strand of the original narrative alive, we could have Edgar (when he discovers Conor is standing) declaring his intention to stand as a Unionist against Conor; or, which is what I prefer, this is where we use the Easter Rising news which will come through at one point in the narrative. When Edgar learns what is happening in Dublin, what I think should happen, is that

Edgar, being the incredibly smart and devious bastard that he is, indulges a little bit of historical clairvoyance. When the news comes through he sees what is going to happen; he sees the Rising will be crushed, the leaders will be executed and that this, in turn, will lead to a renaissance in the fortunes of Sinn Féin. In a word, Edgar should see that the fortunes of the gradualist, democratic, vaguely Anglophile Conor, and the Irish Parliamentry party to which Conor has nailed his colours, are going to be destroyed for ever by what happens in the GPO in Dublin. And if I've understood our conversations correctly, you're not looking for a play about 1916; you're looking for Strindberg re-located in Ireland, but with some familiar Irish political elements in the background. The best way to express what I'm proposing is that we use Ireland and Irish history here, rather in the way Neil Jordan used the border and the Troubles in 'Angel'. He took them but then, on top of the known, he laid a set a complex characters; the pleasure watching the film was watching the characters and the 'Troubles' were just the scenerey. Ditto here; the pleasure for an audience will be watching our characters try to destroy one another with Irish history at a decent remove in the background.

A further point, which connects to what I've just said. By having the psychological drama in the foreground and the history in the background, and by having the historical events which are ongoing as something which the characters use as weapons, I think what will result for the audience will be a fantastic sense of dramatic irony rather like the irony generated by Chekhov in 'The Cherry Orchard'. The audience will know that what Edgar predicts is right; Conor and his gradualist Castle Catholic world is about to end. Yet Conor (and Alice) don't know this because they're so caught up in the emotional maelstrom generated by Edgar; and then on top of this irony comes the next irony, which is that it's Edgar who loses out in the end. Alice and Conor (the Catholics) outmanoeuvre Edgar; the Colonel deserts Edgar; and Edgar dies. However, it's not politics that kills Edgar—this is important—it's conflict and emotional failure and disaster that kill him—but of course an audience will also know that the Rising signalled the end of his British Ireland, his United Kingdom. In a long, roundabout way, I'm trying to say that our audience may see Edgar's fate as a comment on the fate of all Unionist-minded Irishmen but this is not a point I intend to ram down an audience's throat.

The Edgar story has two parts, but two parts which connect. He wants to get one over on Conor and Alice because of what happened in *Part One*. One of the means of doing this is through the share issue scam. The other reason he wants to trounce Conor is Judith. He wants Aidan away so the field is clear for the Colonel. Now we never see the Colonel; we don't know what the Colonel is like, and for all we know the Colonel could be gay and not remotely interested in Judith. I think there's something faintly ridiculous about Edgar's ambition for his daughter— his scheme is a bit loopy—and I want not just to retain but to accent that. It seems (to me) fantastically Edgarish that he thinks he can marry off his daughter to his commanding officer. The improbability of Edgar's plot is part of its joy; there's something ridiculously farce-like about it.

Now into this part of the plot, which is all very creaky and melodramatic, Strindberg has added in Lieutenant Johnston and Alice's two letters and so on. There's a lot of coming and going and much sobbing on sofas, etc cetera. I think the two letters are confusing and we never follow up on the second one (written to the Colonel, I think). What I do like, however, in the midst of this is the two handkerchiefs gag, and the way Alice relieves the Lieutenent of his. I think this section of the play requires cutting and simplifying and should focus on Alice's determination to get Johnston and Aidan to become friends as a way of helping Aidan to cope with heartbreak. I think the story that then develops is that of Alice (with some help from Conor) working for peace in the house, while Edgar is working to destroy Conor and bring the Colonel to the island. For a while it should look as though Edgar will win; Conor is destroyed financially, his chances of electoral triumph are destroyed by the Rising, he loses his job and, adding insult to injury, Edgar is appointed the new Quarantine Officer, and finally, Aidan, his son (due to Edgar's scheming) is posted abroad (the Somme? the Dardenelles?) However, Judith, having discovered what her feelings are for Aidan (this story is run in parallel to the above), then makes her 'impertinent telephone call' (perhaps we should actually see this—after all there is now a telephone on stage) and Edgar's plot crashes like a house of cards; he is destroyed and he dies. The trick, will be to keep the atmosphere of Strindbergian frenzy without degenerating into febrile melodrama. It's the end of Act One, scene one, and the start of Act One, scene two, where these difficulties are most in evidence. Act Two (apart from Judith's illness) is really not too bad (in my judgement).

Finally, I think this should be a play with a lot of scenes and activity, but broken up (rather than run as seamless narrative) and there should also be the sense that in the breaks time passes. Thus, for example, on page 131 of Meyer, after Aidan and the Lieutenant go off with the letter for Judith, if there's a complete break, we can then take Conor's appearance with news of the anonymous letter far more readily and more easily if we think that a day has passed, than is the case at the moment when we are meant to accept that as Aidan and the Lieutenant leave, Conor comes in. (As it happens, I think I may drop the anonymous letter Conor receives but that's a completely different story; alternatively, it did strike me that the anonymous letter could have been written by Alice in order to spur Conor into action: I will pursue this line although I don't know if it will work).

Now, the question is what do I do next? I haven't got a complete narrative worked out for *Part Two* but I do have the sense that it'll be Strindberg simplified, Hibernised and Géblerised. You felt, when we talked in your house, that I should go through *Part One* with the Swedish translation in my hand and then jump into *Part Two*; my present feeling is that I want to jump into *Part Two* and continue what I'm doing in the way that I'm doing it—translating but in places simplifying and adding— until I've got to say the half way mark, at which point I'll know that I'm on track and what my story is. (I'll then be able to write you a synopsis). Then I want to go back to *Part One*, speed through it, and then push through to the end of *Part Two*; what I'm trying to say is, my main concern at the moment is that I'm still not clear about what exactly the story is in *Part Two* and that it is by actually working with the text, sentence by sentence that the story is emerging. I'm not at the moment, at any rate, ready to sit down and produce a fluent synopsis.

So, some questions. I think I should push on with *Part Two* and try and get some more story sorted. Do you agree with me? I'm also more than happy to show you what I've done with *Part Two* (about ten pages) which would be useful if you want a sense of how much more quickly I'm getting the text going now.

You may be on holiday—I don't know; anyway, it doesn't matter if you are because I've got plenty of reading and thinking to keep me busy until you return.

I'm sorry this is such a monstrously long letter but to be able to write at length like this is incredibly helpful (and part of the process). It is not only incredibly important to keep you abreast of progress but also it is incredibly helpful to me to have to put my thoughts down in a logical way on paper like this. This letter is helping me to work the thing out.

I'm glad you're enjoying *W9* although I don't know if 'enjoying' is the right word; my goodness but they are stories of incredible bleakness. I wish I had a lighter, comic touch but unfortunately I didn't get those cards when I got dealt my hand by God. I am enjoying this Strindberg project so hugely (for which I thank you) and mindful of my natural pre-disposition to melancholy and the importance of humour to an audience, I am definitely trying to get some laughs into *Part Two* (and *Part One*).

That is it; this letter is now finished. It must stop.

WARMEST WISHES FROM HERE, SORRY TO INFLICT THIS ON YOU

Carlo

LETTER 4

14th August, 1997

Dear Nicolas,

If *Dance of Death, Part One* and *Part Two* were to play in one evening, how long should each part be? An hour and a half each? And if they were to be that long each, is there an established way of calculating how many pages it will take to play that amount of time? I know with film scripts that conventional lay out with dialogue will play one minute, so a ninety page script plays an hour and a half. Is there a similiar system in the theatre?

I'm away Friday 15th August in Belfast but back home after that.

Best wishes

Carlo

LETTER 5

23rd September, 1997

Dear Nicolas,

A quick line to let you know that I have just got to the end of the first draft of *Dance of Death, Part Two* and I printed it out just a moment ago. For balance I've made it a two act play with two scenes in each act, rather than a one act play with just three scenes.. There's also a good deal of me in it now—indeed, the closer I got to the end of the play the less Strindberg and the more Gébler I found myself putting it. However, I hope I've managed to retain Strindberg's emotional truthfulness and the volatility of his characters. I've certainly tried to do this and we shall see if I've managed it. It would be a crime to just clean Strindberg up. I've also put in some politics—the Easter Rising and the subsequent executions of the leaders. In a funny way, with the politics put in (and the politics are only sketched in—I haven't put them in in a heavy handed way) it's almost now as if the central relationship—Edgar/Alice and their bad marriage— is a metaphor for the relationship of England and Ireland and that bad marriage. Looked at in this light, Alice's behaviour and the struggle for independence become synomonous, and although both are inevitable, within the action of the play neither is seen as entirely admirable or marvellous.

I now propose to go back to the start of *Part One* and will begin cutting and work through both texts until I get to the end of *Part Two*. The Swedish text of *Part One* is 18,480 wds. long; and my version is 20,478 words long; the Swedish text of *Part Two* is 12,320 and mine is 13,349. I shall certainly get my texts down to the length of the Swedish texts, at the very least; perhaps I can get my versions even shorter. One question, however; does it worry you, however, that *Part One* will always be a good bit longer than *Part Two*?

When I've finished cutting I propose (a la Kipling) to let the pieces marinade in my bottom desk drawer for a while. Then I'll have a final, final comb thro' 'em and then I'll get 'em off to you.

Rarely does a writer ever have as much fun as I've been having these last few months. Thank you for making it all possible.

Warmest wishes

Carlo

LETTER 6

13th October, 1997

Dear Nicolas,

I'm going to write this quick so I can get this (and the plays) in the post tonight.

Here is a new (revised) draft of *Dance of Death, Part One* and a draft of *Dance of Death, Part Two*. This may be the first draft of *Part Two* that you've seen but you should know I've been through it a few times.

Both plays are about the same length both in pages and in the number of words. According to my calculations they'd each take (in a no-frills production) about an hour-and-a-half to play *without* an intermission. I've tried to organise things so there's a break at about the forty-five minute point in each play and so I've suggested where the curtain could come at the midway point in each. In both plays this break point is in the middle of the first act, rather than in the gap between the first and second acts, but I think it'll work, or I hope it'll work, and I hope you'll agree with me.

Technical over—and now to the much more important point—the content of *Dance of Death, Part Two*. I hope you think I've gone far enough. I've tried to keep some Strindberg but I have altered, added, enhanced, beefed up, re-written at every turn. Although in my version of *Dance of Death, Part Two* there are parts which won't seem all that different from, say, Meyer, I have in fact changed 60 per cent of the sentences (that is to say I've changed Strindberg's original meaning) while adding a large amount of new material. The question is—does it go far enough? have I gone far enough for you. I'll go further, with pleasure but it seemed to me in writing what you have in front of you that one (I), couldn't go too far away from the original Strindbergian creations; after all, they have a kind of internal coherence; and so, what I hope I've done, what I believe I've done, is to enhance that original internal coherence, by re-writing, cutting, revising, adding and moving scenes. Thus, the *Dance of Death, Part Two* though different is the same story—the story of a poisoned marriage in a poisonous garrison which ends with the death of the husband and the elopement (which is my addition) of the daughter after she has destroyed her father for ever in the eyes of the Colonel whom he, the Captain, so admires. What gives the Colonel sub-plot more complexity and poignancy is the fact that the Captain thinks he is acting independently in trying to marry Judith off; he fails to realise that Alice (in this at least, although for different reasons) is on his side in wanting to get Judith married off and it's Judith, of course, who baulks and who makes the telephone call to the Colonel that destroys her father. Obviously, the Captain never tells Alice about his plans for Judith (Alice overhears these) because the marriage is so awful—and what better indication of its awfulness than that the protagonists cannot reveal to one another that they have the same aspirations for their daughter.

The other thread in the narrative are the events of the rising in Dublin, Easter, 1916. With their introduction in the second act (and I hope I haven't been too heavy handed) I think what will happen for the viewer in the auditorium is that the marriage of Alice and Edgar will come to seem (or will seem) like the bad marriage of England and Ireland. But there is also another theme and it is that victory is never clean—it's always equivocal. The Easter 1916 Rising (although defeated) was the start of an eventually successful campaign which in effect led to the 'divorce' of England and Ireland, and what happens in the play is another defeat and divorce—that of Edgar and Alice; the two are meant to mirror one another, of course, as I've said; but there's also meant to be the suggestion (lurking in the margins of the story) that victory is never entirely wonderful. Those who won the Free State in 1921 were not an entirely wonderful group, and similarly, we should not feel, at the end (in my opinion at any rate) entirely jubilant at the sight of Alice's victory. And by the way, what I had in mind (or hoped to suggest to the audience) with the very end is that Alice, when she links Conor, is actually taking possession of him; in my mind, she is going to marry Conor, or at least she is about to become his lover. So in terms of the through story from *Dance of Death, Part One* the audience should leave at the end of *Part Two* thinking that Alice and Conor had always been attracted, were attracted from when they were children, and therefore the *real* reason Conor came to take the job on Crookedstone (although he didn't admit this to himself) was so that he could 'steal' Alice (which furthermore is also the real reason for Edgar's hostility—unconsciously, at least, the Captain has always know that Conor has wanted Alice.) On one level one could say that the *Dance of Death, Part One and Part Two* taken together, is the story of successful adultery in which neither of the parties (Alice and Conor) know what they are doing. Although they might both admit that they have lustful feelings for one another, neither are ever prepared to admit that their feelings are as long lasting and deep as they are.

I think I've gone on long enough. I'm sure there'll be lots more to discuss when you've read the enclosed. You can get me at home any day (including weekends—and I'm happy to be called at any time) except Friday when I'm in HMP Maghaberry where I'm the writer-in-residence (God help me!)

Again, again, again, thank you for getting me to do this.

With warmest wishes

Carlo

PS: I rang the Strindberg expert as you suggested many, many times but I never got a reply.

LETTER 7

13th October, 1997

Dear Nicolas,

I enclose final drafts of Parts *One* and *Two*.

In the case of *Part One*, the changes are infinitesimal. I have put in the reference about the Liffey freezing and made a half-line allusion to the Dawson family ménage moving south to Dublin so Edgar (aged fourteen) can teach. I have also changed the name of Doctor Haverty's wife from Geraldine to Maureen as it has just occurred to me that my own doctor has a wife called Geraldine. This might be an act of over-zealous punctiliousness on my part, but what the hell. I have also made a few other small additions and alterations, inc. one to the end (which I hope you like).

I am absolutely certain, by the way, that altering *Part One* as we discussed (in our last telephone conversation) so that Edgar comes to Dublin to teach as an adolescent, is absolutely right. Yes, it means we will only have one Ulster accent in the cast (the Captain) but also it fits aesthetically and thematically as it suggests that, right from the start of his life, Edgar was always rootless and peripatetic.

I now regard the text as almost definitely finished—or at least as finished as anything ever is until rehearsals commence.

Part Two is more substantially altered, along the lines that we discussed in the Crown. I have cut six pages as you asked, thus slimming the text down from 51 to 46 pages. I have also taken out nearly all the stuff about Edgar as a vampire and substituted the Freudian story as we discussed; one, Edgar has never forgiven Conor for almost stealing his wife; two, Edgar resents Aidan's interest in Judith (he sees a pattern); Edgar's response to these feelings is that he determines to bankrupt Conor, economically, socially and any other way he can.

But before I go into what the Captain does, I think it's important to re-cap on the Edgar/Alice/Conor back story.

Alice has always liked Conor and vice versa. They have known one another since childhood. They have not been lovers but (and this is what I think is buried in the play, this is, in fact, the dramatic crux of the play) during adolescence there have been fumblings; Conor has put his hands where he oughtn't to have put them, and furthermore, Alice and Conor have been in love. At that stage Alice had assumed she would marry Conor, her cousin; but then the Captain (who had come south and whom she had first seen on a freezing winter morning) had burst into her life and swept her off her feet. So, she had renounced Conor and had married Edgar.

Conor, then, and with much chagrin, himself marries and subsequently divorces (a separation made more acrimonious by the Captain's meddling). After the divorce, Conor goes to America where mysterious things happen (he makes his money, illegally, I think) and then Conor returns to Ireland, finding a job (because he still hankers after Alice, his childhood sweetheart) on Crookedstone, as Quarantine Master.

Within hours of re-meeting, Conor and Alice are hormonally excited (they have the hots for each other); something nearly happens (at the end of *Part One*) but then it doesn't. (What happens, of course, is that Conor sees what a monster Alice is and how he is ultimately insignificant in relation to the *folie à deux* which characterises the relationship of the Captain and Alice).

And yet, and yet, Conor's feeling for Alice never dies, either, nor do hers for him. The Captain knows this and so, in *Part Two*, he sets out to destroy, to bankrupt in every way possible his rival.

Now the way the Captain manages to do this involves a good deal of luck; he doesn't, of course, set the collapse of the Donegal Lime Company in motion; that's happenstance but it's the opportunity he has being waiting for for years. (Remember also, he's extracted all the useful info. he's ever going to get out of Conor regarding quarantine in Portugal). The collapse of Donegal Lime happens to coincide with the point at which the Captain realises he won't get anything more out of

Conor.

The Captain's assault on Conor goes like this; when Donegal Lime begins to totter, the Captain doesn't tell Conor to get his money out because collapse is coming; he let's Conor go down with the sinking company. Then, having bankrupted the man, he is able, in quick succession, to achieve two other coups which he finesses simultaneously and which, incidentally, are bound up with the Colonel with whom he is dealing in relation to Judith. One, he has Aidan sent away supported by charitable funds organised by the Colonel which has the side effect of spoiling Conor's likely electoral success, and two, (which, as I say, is all bound up with his Judith strategy) he has the Colonel appoint him, the Captain, Inspector of Quarantine, i.e. he gets himself made into Conor's boss. (Or least this is how the Captain sees it; the role may be an honorific—it doesn't matter.)

Meanwhile, in tandem with the above, we have Aidan chasing Judith, and Judith chasing Aidan, and Alice (besides skirmishing with the Captain continuously) trying to help Aidan, who she rather pities but with whom she does not ultimately sympathize. Like the Captain (and she's as bad as Edgar is in this respect) she also sees old Colonel Beggs as Judith's best and most profitable route out of Crookedstone, poverty and the bitchiness of garrison life. Alice is absolutely not in dispute with her husband about Judith's future; she's as bad (or calculating) as he is, as I said. The only differences between the Captain and Alice are as regards the Coynes; Alice, unlike the Captain, does not fear Aidan; she knows him for what he is, a rather nice but innocent and naive young man; she doesn't want Judith to hurt him, particularly as (in her, Alice's, mind) the Colonel thing is going to happen and then Aidan's really going to get hurt. So she tries to help Aidan; among other things she persuades him to be friends with Johnston.

The other big difference between the Captain and Alice (and here lies, as I've said, the dramatic crux of the play) concerns Conor. It's the motor at the heart of it all. Alice is bound by indissoluble bands to the Captain but Conor provokes long forgotten feelings of desire. Nothing, of course, under ordinary circs. would ever happen between Alice and Conor; Alice is too bound up with Edgar to ever leave him and Conor is too circumspect to steal Alice, but of course the Captain can't stop himself from meddling and taking revenge and so precipitates the very last thing he wants in the world—he drives Judith into Aidan's arms, which in turn kills him, and which in turn leaves Alice free to take Conor. If the play has a moral, it is that the Captain should have done nothing and then he'd have got his way on every front. Alice would have stayed with him and maybe Judith would have chosen the Colonel.

I have made Judith eighteen or twenty, by the way, to give greater latitude in casting. I have placed her boarding school in Dublin not Derry and, like Alice (and Conor) she has a refined Dublin accent.

Yes, Johnston is English. And yes, Jack Davenport would be brilliant— so brilliant I wonder if he could play Aidan? I know it's all a matter of mastering the accent.

You wondered when we last spoke if I am excited. Well, yes, I am incredibly excited although I am trying to keep myself on a very tight rein (hence perhaps the feelings don't show). There is also another really important thing on my mind (perhaps also inhibiting the showing of feelings of excitement) and that is a huge sense a) that this is a colossal privilege (lines by me will be said on a stage) and b) that what really matters now (because so much rides on this and that includes, to some extent, the economic well-being of the Tricycle) that I must get the texts of the two plays right. That's my task, and, as far as I'm able, that's what I must ensure. To this end I have thus been over and over and over the plays and I do feel that I have arrived somewhere, at last. I think they have a shape, and a beginning and a middle and an end, and I hope they are actable. I also think *Part Two* will stand without *Part One*; there are enough dark hints in it for an audience to keep watching. I will of course do any more that needs doing and I hope, now you have both parts in your hands, you too will agree that a stage, close to if not actually the end (because there is no end in writing), has been reached.

I have loved doing this.

The most useful translations were Eight Best Plays, August Strindberg, translated by Edwin Björkman and N. Erichsen (with an intro. by Alan Harris). Duckworth, London, 1950 & 1978; Dramas of Testimony, August Strindberg, trans. and intro. by Walter Johnson, University of Washington Press, Seattle and London, 1975.

I hope this finds you in tip-top form.

Warmest wishes

Carlo

LETTER 8

10th December, 1997

Dear Nicolas,

Some random thoughts in no particular order:

The seasons. I've set *Part One* in 1913 (as discussed) in October, when the autumn is well on in the west of Ireland. It could even be November if you thought that was better, more autumnal. *Part Two*, as before, takes place at Easter.

Title and description. According to my OED, 'version' means a 'new translation'; could I suggest, therefore, we call *Part One*, 'a new version' (which I think is better than 'a new translation'), and that we call *Part Two*, 'a new free version'. Or is that wishy-washy? It could be 'A new free version based on (or inspired by) Strindberg's play, *Dance of Death, Part Two* if you think the frontispiece description needs more meat. The other way to describe *Part Two* would be to call it a new free interpretation (or some variation of these words). What do you think of that? I've left it at version and free version but would be happy to change to the alternative.

Your question: How much is Gébler in *Part Two* and how much is Strindberg is hard to answer. I'd say it's about half me, half him, or maybe even a bit more me, although I have obviously tried to make *me fit him*; I've self-consciously written in his style. Also, the story is his story; Judith, the Captain's daughter, bucks the Captain's plans by falling for Aidan and rejecting the Colonel. What is new is that she absconds with Aidan in my version; all the Easter 1916 stuff is new; the syndicate stuff is also new although the linking of the collapse of a company and Conor's downfall does come from Strindberg. Also new is the poison letter and the way Alice kills the Captain by reading Judith's letter out to him. I've also altered the emphasis of the scene where Alice takes Judith's tokens (lace handkerchiefs) from Aidan and Johnston. So there's quite a bit that's new in other words, but what has been retained (I believe) in the story is the moral (young generation bucks the trend of older generation) and Strindberg's beautiful emotional fluency.

Next, Meyer. You wondered whether to read the Meyer or not? I think at some point it might be useful(ish) as some journalist in the future is bound to ask how this (my version) compares with the original. Or you can just quote the above para. and save yourself the trouble.

A quibble. *Part One*, you want 'trouble never comes in a single platoon'. I have to say, I still prefer, 'trouble never comes in single file but always in battalions' which we had before and which was my west of Ireland grandmother's saying. I think the logic is military; men moving in single file can be picked off one at a time, whereas a battalion, a mass of men, cannot be picked off; a battalion will always overwhelm you.

Tennis. In the Meyer, Judith comes in and says, 'Why won't you come and play tennis?' In the Swedish she says, 'Will you come and play tennis'. 'Anyone for tennis?' is my invention.

Judith. Here are some thoughts on her:

Of course, to understand the character and because we are Freudians, we have to go to the parents. It's like this:

In *Part One*, Alice boasts to Conor about her chapped hands and ragged nails, et cetera; she maintains this is the consequence of her having to be the domestic drudge. This is at best an exaggeration, if not a downright lie; the servants have been doing the housework until just before Conor's arrival and they have only just left. Alice hasn't been doing any drudging lately—but then she's never one to let the truth get in the way of a good moan.

A couple of pages later, on page 22, the Captain tells Conor that he feels as if he's fallen off the battlements and into the sea. He wants Conor's sympathy and is playing up his illness.[1] But as soon as Conor leaves, on page 23, the Captain makes an amazing recovery, and within seconds is talking to Alice. 'How nice Conor is,' he says, 'I'd forgotten.'

I'm taking a long time about this but what I'm getting at is that Edgar and Alice are both spoofers, performers; they can turn an act on and off like a tap, particularly when they want to get someone's sympathy. They are also liars, fantasists and dreamers.

This is the atmosphere then, in which Judith (and her brother who sinks from sight in *Part Two*—does that matter by the way?) grow up. As a child, Judith finds it charming; her parents are so theatrical, so playful, so intriguing; they love to put on voices and strike poses; but as Judith grows older (eight, nine, ten) the attractions of parental play acting begin to pall. Behind the froth, as Judith begins to see with greater and greater clarity, there lie unpleasant and disagreeable motives. Judith sees these and begins to feel that her parents, in their performances, are trying in their separate ways to enlist her on their side. This is true; they are. But this endless appeal to Judith to take one side or the other, is of course something she hates—any child would hate this in fact because special pleading threatens the most cherished ambition of all children (no matter how warped the home) which is the equal love of both parents and a happy harmonious family, and both pa and ma at home. (I certainly know from my own experience in childhood, although it took years of shrinkage to get this out, that though my father was a monster I wanted him and my mother to be together, I did not want them to divorce—even though I recognised it was inevitable). Even though my father was a monster what the child, Carlo, wanted, was Mum and Dad living together with me (and with of course both of them loving me).

Back to the play; to their credit, Alice and Edgar also both recognise that what they are doing to Judith—asking her to chose between them in effect—is going to harm her (which suggests an extraordinary degree of knowing self-consciousness on their part). Their response (since they're incapable of reforming themselves—they are very selfish as well as being very perceptive people) is to send Judith and her brother away during adolescence, and I would imagine that when this happens, Judith and her brother are *delighted* to be out of the hothouse that is home.

Now the effect of all this on Judith, is that she is, in some sense, like

them. How could she not be like them? And she is like them in the key
sense that there is something of the performer about her, too. Or to put
it in a different way, there is a bit of her that is always somehow above
events and monitoring events, whilst the rest of her personality, although
apparently engaged, is trying out what she is doing; and the bit of her
that's above keeps an eye on the rest of her and what she is trying out. Let
me put this really simply; when she's with Aidan, she's flirty (she likes
him) but she's also playing at being flirty (and watching herself playing
at being flirty) none of which compromises the authentic feelings she has
for Aidan.

The trajectory of Judith's story in *Part Two* is the age old one of
heroines from time immemorial; as a result of pain she learns what she
sincerely feels, and having learnt the truth about her feelings, she is able
to act and run away with Aidan.

Aidan. His background, I think, is simpler and sadder. Conor loves
Alice. Alice is going to marry Conor. Then up pops the Captain. Alice
marries the Captain. On the rebound, Conor marries Karen. His wife is
a neurotic, sexless, pious, joyless nightmare. Relations deteriorate to
such an extent a divorce is inevitable. Conor agrees that the grounds for
this will be his adultery (which of course isn't true. He just has to say he's
been unfaithful in order to get the divorce). After the divorce, a shaming
thing in late-Victorian Ireland, Conor has to go to America where he stays
for fourteen or fifteen years. (He can only return when his case has been
forgotten, which is only a little before his arrival on Crookedstone. His
alienation from the Catholic community would also make him more
likely to seek a government job).

While Conor is in America, Aidan has to live with his mother; his
childhood is unhappy and lonely; his life has no colour or joy. At fifteen
he wangles a place at the Cadet School in Derry. His mother, who is a
snob, acquiesces. Enter the Captain (with whom she has already had
dealings fifteen years earlier when she was seeking custody of her
children). The Capt. cloaks his offer to coach Aidan as a way of hitting
and hurting Conor. Karen is delighted to go along with this since, having
brooded on her divorce for fifteen miserable years, she has now convinced
herself that Conor really did commit adultery. (Like the Captain she's a
fantasist who eventually believes her own delusions).

Aidan moves to Crookedstone and his hormones start to fizz. (Judith
is the cause of this.) He also realises that everything his mother has told
him about Conor over the previous fifteen years is skewed by hatred.
Aidan's story in the play is that of the immature hero, parked on the edge
of life and longing to get involved. When Judith comes to the quayside,
he is the one (I think) who says, come on, come with me, and he takes her
off with him. By performing this action he moves from immaturity to

maturity, he moves from being an on-looker to being an active participator in life (his decision to act being based on his feelings not his thoughts). This is not in the play as we see it (there ain't room for everything) but this is how I imagine it. And perhaps the actor playing Aidan should be told this.

Will you want double-space copies for rehearsals? When everything's finished (literals eliminated, et cetera) I could send you a disc that you could print drafts from.

I think your suggestions regarding *Part Two* all work magnificently. I hope you like the photograph conceit. If not, well, we could make it just a photograph for Easter.

Warmest wishes

Carlo

[1] And it must also be remembered that, as well as being a lifelong hypochondriac, the Captain is also old and unwell and his body is running down.

LETTER 9

Wednesday 31st December, 1997

Dear Nicolas,

The play overall is also more or less what it was before; so you needn't plough through it; I've only made v. small changes. However, what you should know, is that in the first Johnston/Aidan interchange (they're waiting while Alice writes the letter) I've restored 'hot'. It seems to me that Ireland is never hot (especially at Easter) so for them to agree it's hot is clearly an indication that they're each only saying the first thing that comes into their heads, i.e. "Gosh, it's hot!" I have also re-written all the French door references throughout in order to emphasise the idea that any French door action takes place right at the French doors and to minimise the impression that the action takes place on an extended balcony-cum-battlement that stretches for several miles beyond the French doors. Of course there isn't room for such a battlement; I've taken that point very much on board. And while we're on the subject of the French doors, the Capt. should die (in my opinion) just on the far side of the doors, i.e. just out of the room—and not at the end of a battlement.

I can't think of anything else to say right now. I look forward to hearing your response. I believe I've done it this time.

Have you had a good time in SA?
Warmest wishes

Carlo

LETTER 10

Friday 2nd January, 1998

Dear Nicolas,

My first letter of the new year. Since sending you the script on New Year's Eve, I've had some more thoughts about *Dance of Death,Part Two* and I thought you should have these as well as the new draft. So here they are, in particular order of importance.

First, I want to expand on how I got to what you have. What this draft represents is the best of the 2nd draft and the best of the draft that I sent you after that (the one that you thought was too plotty). In other words, in the draft you have in front of you, you have the simplicities of the opening scene pacé draft 2, and the advances of the plotty draft (which doesn't have a number) combined together to make what I hope is a final draft and which, for our purposes, I have called draft 3. (The plotty draft doesn't have a number).

You were right, the plotty draft was too plotty in relation to the Captain subterfuge and it is better to suggest the coming story with a couple of straightforward allusions (although to an audience these will seem a little mysterious to begin with) rather than have a long, expositionary conversation between Alice and the Captain. I think sometimes a writer— at least this writer (me)—becomes so intimate, and so familiar with material, that the curse of over-writing kicks. One (I) are so determined that absolutely everything will be understood, there is tendency to cross t's and dot i's, and an unwillingness (or a reluctance) to allow a couple of straight-forward allusions to do the work. Anyway, this is a very long way of saying that I think the Donegal Lime subplot is now firmly but delicately and unplottily in place. It now has, Donegal Lime sub-plot wise, just the right amount of material—enough to make the story clear, but not so much as to overwhelm a viewer or audience member.

You should also know that the means by which I arrived at the draft you have in front of you are as we discussed; I put the ms. in a drawer, I let the text marinade. And then, before, during and after Christmas, I got it out each day, read the thing from start to finish (trying to put myself in the position of someone in the audience) and then made a few unhurried changes during each trawl through. I tried, in other words, not to read the play as a writer, but to look at the whole play with fresh eyes each day much as a member of an audience might see it. And I succeeded, I think, because I only gave it forty five minutes of my time each time, rather than the whole day, which would be my usual working pattern.

You should also know that I have made a few other small changes to the text (as I said in the letter that accompanies the ms.) but these are matters of detail not substance. The play's the same—you don't have to read the whole damned thing again to get a handle on the Donegal Lime sub-plot.

I thought you might also like to know my handle on the background or back story to the Donegal Lime sub-plot. It's like this: for some time, the Captain has known that Donegal Lime is going to fold; Ha! he thinks, now I can destroy Conor for trying to steal Alice, et cetera. He sells most *but not all* of his shares—it is imperative that it appears to the other members of the garrison that he loses just as they do. He then deliberately does not tell either Conor or the other members of the syndicate that the company is ailing. Instead, in the weeks just before Easter, he confines himself to poisoning the atmosphere—that is to say, he dedicates himself to altering the attitude of the junior officers in the garrison towards Conor. Now the way he actually does this is subtle and very unstraight-forward. He doesn't go around saying that Conor's a bastard, he won't give money, if he doesn't give money, we'll collapse. Oh no. What he does (and the play is full of references to this) is that he makes it his business to let the junior officers know how 'hurt' he is by Conor's lack of generosity. 'Oh that blasted, fellow Conor,' his argument probably runs, 'Here he is on Crookedstone; I brought him here; I got him the job; I helped him; I got his son out of the clutches of Conor's wretched ex-wife; I'm tutoring this stupid boy, in my own time and at my expense so that he can pass the exam and go to the Royal Academy at Woolwich; and how does this blasted man re-pay my generosity and my kindness? By declining to subscribe any more funds to Donegal Lime just at the time the company needs the money most. He's a selfish, ungenerous, uncharitable egomaniac who's forgotten who his real friends are, et cetera.' When we see the Captain, as we do throughout the play, endlessly ticking Conor off for his failure to thank him (the Captain) properly as regards everything he has done for him (Conor),what we are seeing is the Captain's rhetoric in the mess re-couched in a different form; we're getting a glimpse of the bee the Captain has in his bonnet. The Captain is an obsessive and an hysteric; at the moment the play occurs, all that he is eating and breathing and drinking is Conor's infidelity, ingratitude and betrayal; it's the stuff of the Captain's being; he's pumping it out twenty-four hours a day and when he's in contact with Conor and Alice, he can't help but keep it up. So Conor too, gets the Captain's line about Conor's ingratitude, just as all the officers in the mess have got it. My

point (and sorry to labour it) is that when the Captain is in destruction-
mode, the fingerprints of his intentions (forgive the clumsy metaphor)
are all over his language and his discourse. That's why he keeps banging
on about Conor's failure to thank him properly, and conversely, the
proper gratitude shown by the junior officers, for instance, who buy him
a hideous oil painting the first time he retires. It is this that Alice picks up
on—as she would, she's been living with him for twenty-seven years and
has presumably known him for longer. When she hears the Capt. talk to
Judith at the end of Act I, Scene 1 about Conor being always on the take,
she recognises at once that a storm is coming and sets about trying to find
Conor at once.

A word now about the poison letter. It's doggerel with a semi-
Limerick-like structure. I struggled long and hard with this and worried
whether the ditty shouldn't be more sophisticated. But then, in the end,
I decided no, it should be crude, and for two reasons. One, I had a look
at some poison letters from the period—and was reminded that they
were always banal; they were, I was reminded (and indeed still are, for
they remain a popular feature of Irish political life) the equivalent of
graffiti on a lavatory wall. I also concluded that this banality, far from
being an indication of the creator's low level of intelligence, was in fact
very much part of the power of poison letters. Because they seem to have
been written by Caliban, the poisoned letters that litter Irish history, carry
considerably more threat than they would have carried had they seemed
to spring from the pen of Ariel. And as a final rider to this, a little story
which I hope throws some light on military crudity. Some years ago, a
British politician (Neil Kinnock?) went to visit a British Army regiment
at their barracks in Belfast and, according to the hacks covering the visit
(not to mention the Belfast rumour machine), there was a picture on the
wall of the Mess of dead people killed by soliders of the regiment with,
stuck across it, 'Stopped by the A Team' complete with cutout photographs
of characters from the hit TV series with the faces of soldiers from
regiment superimposed on them. It was an incredibly stupid, asinine
example of barrack room bravado and so, in its different way, is the vile
limerick Conor receives with its attempt to connect political treachery
and a refusal to give further financial aid.

I've had a nice Christmas but a lot of work; the play took some time
(I'm not complaining, I liked working on it, and I know it's critical that
the work is absolutely right) but what really took the lion's share of my
time were the proofs of my novel, *How to Murder a Man*; they arrived on
the 23rd December, with a letter asking me to have 'em back to the
publisher, marked up, et cetera, by Monday 5th January, 1998. (I love
publishers.) I have finished them anyway, and they went off with the play.
I also had to write some journalism, inc. a review of Fintan O'Toole's

rather good biography of Richard Brinsley Sheridan. Tyga is rather big, and the pregnancy still rather worrying; she is not allowed to be further than five miles from the hospital and the gynacologist's last words to her before Christmas were, "You have a time bomb in you." (I love doctors.) Editing the film starts next week—but the editor is coming here (with his Avid) as I don't want to be away from Tyga at all. And—no doubt the biggest news of all—we have a puppy whom the children have called Tessa.

Warmest from here

Carlo

LETTER 11

Saturday 3rd January, 1998

Dear Nicolas,

A rider (addition) to yesterday's fax. The posters in west Belfast 'Drug Dealers Beware—You have one day to go,' and the handwritten death notices and poison warnings I have seen, taken from shops in Twinbrook, all have fantastic evil energy. They're also disgusting crude, naff, naive, artless, infantile—the product of an intelligence that is not an intelligence. The naffness of Ulster poison letters and warnings are crucial to their power to terrify. The sub-Limerick Conor receives is a chip off the same block.

Warmest

Carlo

LETTER 12

Saturday 10th January, 1998

Dear Nicolas,

What a relief to know that you like *Part Two* and how kind of you to have read it, and then to have rung me today when you obviously have got a lot on your plate.

I have made the changes we discussed. You simply remove pages 4, 18 and 25 from the draft you have (number three), and insert the enclosed. What could be simpler? The changes were small so the other lines on the page remain unchanged.

I hope your ordeal under the knife has passed off satisfactorily. I am definitely becoming phobic about hospitals.

I look forward to speaking to you in the week about changes to *Part One* and I hope a leading actress drops into your lap (metaphorically).

With warmest wishes

Carlo

LETTER 13

Wednesday 14th January, 1998

Dear Nicolas,

Here are my responses to your questions. New lines that I have suggested I haven't yet incorporated into the text as I imagined we should have a chat first about the practicalities of this. Do we want to just change by hand the last draft of *One* (Dec. 9th 1997) or do I produce a final, final draft? Or what?

1) In my opinion Edgar and Alice married between Christmas and the New Year. They're the type who like to have their big events when all the other big events of the year are happening. They wouldn't, for instance, have ever considered having their wedding in February because in February nothing happens. Oh no, it would have to be December for them. In my mind the day in question is December 30th. As this is autumn, October, even November, there are therefore six, eight, ten weeks to go. In the light of this could I make the following suggestion:

> **CAPTAIN:** Don't be so ignorant. Just six weeks to go. I shall have to lay in some wine for our Silver Wedding—
> **ALICE:** You are joking?
> **CAPTAIN:** No, I'm not.

2) Yes could I suggest the following:

> **CAPTAIN** [*angry*]: Doesn't surprise me ... he's always ingratiating himself with the Colonel ... Think if I'd chosen medicine?

3) How did Maureen (the Doctor's wife) cheat Alice? She didn't—not in the expected sense that she took something from Alice that wasn't hers to take. What Alice is really objecting to (this is my back story) is that Maureen hasn't become her ally, her totally uncritical ally, and because she isn't this, in Alice's book, that makes Maureen a cheat. It's complicated

to go into all of this so what about this (page 6):

> CAPTAIN [*angry*]: Doesn't surprise me ... he's always ingratiating himself with the Colonel ... Think if I'd chosen medicine?
> ALICE [*dealing*]: I thought Maureen was my friend ... well, she wasn't, was she? so critical, so superior -
> CAPTAIN: Ah, they're all like that ... snobs ... what's trumps?

4) What about:

> ALICE [*nostalgic*]: How different my life would be if I'd stayed in the theatre. All the girls I started with are famous now —
> CAPTAIN: Oh no, we're not back on that again, are we? Now I do need a drink, et cetera.

5) Yes, the is missing before Gresham: will re-instate.

6) What about :

> ALICE: You don't talk, you grovel. You do with all inferiors without realising. You might seem the bully, but really, inside, you're a slave.
> CAPTAIN: Very good—
> ALICE: Yet bad as you are with your men, you're far worse with your equals and your superiors. In their company you become a lovesick girl, simpering, swooning, sycophantic—
> CAPTAIN [*as if hurt*]: Ah!

7) Yes, my assumption is that the Grand is in Derry. I don't actually know if there was such a hotel; I also, on reflection think it's not the best name I could come up with. What about the Great Northern? Again, I don't know if there was such a hotel, but those who know Ireland will assume it's a railway hotel (because it echoes 'the Great Southern' which was a real chain). And a railway hotel was exactly the sort of place to cater for a garrison party. Thus we would have:

> ALICE: You know who's cooking for Haverty? The chef from the Great Northern.
> CAPTAIN: I bet grouse is on the menu. Delicious. The world's supreme game bird. Only not if roasted in lard.

8) Well spotted, mon brave. It should be the 'The Walls of Limerick' (not 'the Siege'). 'The Walls of Limerick' is an Irish set dance, and a bog-

standard Irish set dance at that and as likely to have been danced at a Regimental ball as at a GAA function. And it's still with us. At every wedding I go to in Ireland, 'The Walls of Limerick' is always danced. Therefore the text reads:

> **CAPTAIN** [*sitting at the desk*]: Why not? But none of your funeral marches or Oirish laments. No need to underline what I can work out. 'My husband's so horrid. Would I was dead.' Roll drums, sound trumpets, take your partners pl ... ease, for 'The Walls of Limerick'. There's champagne in the pantry. Can we open one ... have a party?

9) A *ménage a trois* yes, but without the sex. What I imagine is that for company and a few extra coppers, at some point in the past, the Captain agreed to billet a soldier, an unmarried junior officer who preferred the idea of married quarters to barracks. At first I imagine the lodger and Mr. and Mrs. Dawson got on famously, but then jealousy reared its ugly head and the Captain accused the lodger of making love to his wife.

We could amend the dialogue to reflect this; could I suggest the following:

> **CAPTAIN:** You're too kind. But can I remind you, we did try it ... and at first, dare I say it, we were happy—
> **ALICE:** Yes, and look what happened, our poor lodger, poor Lieutenant Flynn, he found you quite the Othello, didn't he?—
> **CAPTAIN:** Oh, all right, let's drop it, please.

10) I agree, so what about:

> **CONOR:** Strength isn't everything. You've got to bend. I learnt that in the divorce.

11) Yes, so what about:

> **CAPTAIN:** I'm sorry for him if he can't rely on his own strength. Look, when the body stops, what are you? A load of muck in a wheel barrow, only fit for the garden. But as long as you're alive, you've got to fight and struggle. Sheer effort and a refusal to submit, that's how I got this far.

12) It's ironic; Edgar is describing Conor's ex-wife, Karen as a jewel when what he means is the reverse. So what about:

> **CAPTAIN:** Ah, you too have drunk the bitter cup of matrimony. Damned

women! And yours was an ugly specimen—
CONOR [gently]: I'd rather not talk about her—
CAPTAIN [*correcting himself*]: I mean that lovely jewel of yours ... I suppose
not. Luckily, mine isn't too bad for all her failings—
CONOR [*smiles, in a good-natured way*]: For all her failings!

[Note: Edgar's speech about Alice's tightness should be amended:

CAPTAIN: You've no idea. If money's even a tiny bit tight ... as happens,
occasionally ... and she loves to tell me I'm a bad breadwinner.
CONOR: But you just said you've a big income.

13) What about:

ALICE: He's worse than usual.
CONOR: A bit wobbly?
ALICE: No, much worse than usual!

14) What about:

ALICE: I wish. When we were engaged we broke it off, twice ... and we've
tried to beak it off every day since we married. We did manage it once
... five years ago ... I ran away ... got as far as Londonderry ... spent the
night alone in a hotel ... he came and fetched me the next morning
... but it won't happen again. We're welded together. I realise that
now. Only death can prise us apart.

15) Well, I've always imagined they were having sex, so what about:

ALICE: When you got to the house Edgar and I were out—
CONOR: You couldn't answer the door ... no, you were invited somewhere
... anyway, it doesn't matter now—
ALICE: Conor, listen! When I asked you to eat with us, I thought there
was food. [*Hiding her face in her hands*] But there isn't so much as a crust
of bread. You must think I'm always offering food and failing you—

16) Yes, it should be:

CAPTAIN: On our silver jubilee! Tell me, how does he really seem to you?
He never reveals anything personal about himself. Have you noticed?
ALICE: Yes, but we haven't asked him any personal questions, have we?

17) The maid/cook problem:

ALICE: It'll be rough and ready. The maid's run off but I've still got a cook.

CONOR: Simple suits me.

[ALICE *goes off; later she returns wearing an apron. We presume she's been with cook in kitchen.*]

Then:

ALICE: I can't play with these. Look! Ragged nails. Cracked skin. You know why? Scrubbing pots, hauling coal, ironing, washing—

CONOR: But you said the maid only just left—

ALICE [*knowing she's been caught out*]: Yes ... well ... she has, which is just typical, she has, but they go AWOL all the time ... all the time. They hate us and then I have to skivvy. Now how am I going to get out of supper? Wouldn't it be brilliant if this tower burnt down?

CONOR: Alice! Don't tempt fate.

Then Alice and Edgar discover that Cook has gone, when Alice spots the trunk in the hall.

18) No, Kitty is Cook's name. To make it easy what about:

ALICE: You dug this hole. When was cook last paid? Six months ago!

CAPTAIN: Yes, since when cook has been stealing her wages.

19) Yes, I agree; so what about:

CONOR [*rushing in*]: Edgar ... I've uh ... got some quite good news, mostly. Doctor Haverty says he knows all about your heart ... in fact everyone at the party knew about it—

CAPTAIN: My heart?

20) What about:

CONOR: Won't you take off your boots?

CAPTAIN: I'm a soldier. I must be ready for action at all times.

In answer to your question, in the original, Conor responds to this last line by saying, "Are you expecting a battle?" I changed it to Kaiser because I thought that was topical, and there was great fearfulness at the time regarding a German invasion:

CONOR: Won't you take off your boots?

CAPTAIN: I'm a soldier. I must be ready for action at all times.
CONOR: Kaiser's coming, is he?
CAPTAIN: Maybe. He's coming one day soon. [*Sitting up*] Conor, you are the only person in the world I can ask. If, *when*, I die, look after my children?

21) Yes, what about:

CONOR: Come on, what I've seen tonight, this is hell. [*Silence*]
CAPTAIN: You've no idea. I'm in bits.

22) Yes, how about this:

ALICE [*hearing the front door knocker tapping in the wind*]: Do you hear someone at the front door?
CONOR [*puzzled*]: Was there? Go and see. There's nothing you can do here.
[ALICE *goes out to the porch and opens the front door. No one there. She turns and looks back into the room.*]
CAPTAIN [*waking*]: So is the new Quarantine Officer going to cope?
[ALICE, *seeing the* CAPTAIN *has revived, seizes her chance and goes out, closing the front door behind.*]
CONOR: He'll cope.

23) Yes, what about:

CAPTAIN: Put the flowers in water. [*Opens and reads third telegram.*] I'm not easily taken in and I'm hardly enamoured of the human race, but by God, this comes from the heart! It could come from nowhere else.
ALICE: Fool.

24) Yes, how about:

ALICE: Look at him now! ... blowing a gale and the coat wide open. He must really want to die!

25) Absolutely, it's jokey. Conor is playing at being the Irish broth of a boy. If you don't like, could I suggest the following:

CONOR [*coming in from the porch*]: Good morning, Alice, and what a lovely one, too.

26) Yes, a confusion all right; could I suggest the following:

ALICE: That's difficult. He has a talent for rooting out people's secrets. And I don't know how you could have failed to notice that the minute, no, the second he stopped drinking ... he locked on to you and started asking question after question. Just a few hours of interrogation and he could play you. Amazing. But he's not an actor ... he's a dead man who lives by consuming others ... a cannibal—

27) Yes, what about:

ALICE [*realising suddenly*]: You saw Judith, yesterday? Got the train down.
CAPTAIN: Oh yes.

28) Yes:

CONOR: You're the first woman I've ever felt the slightest bit sorry for ... all the others got what they deserved.

29) No, I suggest we keep it as it is:

ALICE: Then stay ... or he'll beat me, as he has every day of our marriage. He beat me in front of the children. He even threw me in the sea—

This is an exaggeration; Edgar has never hit Alice (although it's true he pushed her in the sea). Edgar inflicts his hurt mentally; he doesn't need to thump her.

30) Yes:

CONOR: Who?
ALICE: The Quarter Master.[1] He knows what Edgar and Sergeant-Major Hibbert have been 'up' to.

31) Yes, change the stage direction:

The CAPTAIN *is pale and tired looking with stubble on his chin. He has changed from his dress back to his service uniform. He sits at the desk playing Patience. He wears his glasses.*

Yes, the blindness is part of his illness. I think we should imagine that in the gap between scenes one and two, his eyes have suddenly got much, much worse. Further thoughts on the start of the scene below.

32) He doesn't throw the wreath away because he knows that to throw Alice's wreath away would be *beyond the pale*. She values her wreaths (a gift from her brother as we later discover) more than anything else in the world.

(The scene that starts with the Captain alone). I've bunched your next three questions together because I'm going to answer them together.

You wondered about the music: Yes, Strindberg refers to interval music accompanying this long section but he doesn't say what it is. (He calls it simply 'interval' music). He also indicates that the music continues until the characters (Alice & Conor) enter. Am I right to presume from your query that you think 'Danny Boy' is a bit naff? So shall we cut it? In fact, I think we should if we want the various sounds that the Captain hears at the start of the scene to carry the significance we want them to carry. Quite simply, McCormack will drown them out.

You are also right that the spooky noise and the tapping of the telegraph aren't properly orchestrated or choreographed.

Finally, I think Alice and Conor have dissembled; they have arrived together but they want to hide the fact from the Captain; and therefore I've altered their entrance to make this clearer.

So, in the light of all these queries of yours and my responses, could I suggest that stage directions at the start of scene 2 are amended to read as follows:

Scene 2

That evening, the same. The SENTRY *is at his post. The laurel wreaths hang over the back of a chair.*

The CAPTAIN *is pale and tired looking with stubble on his chin. He has changed from his dress back to his service uniform. He sits at the desk playing Patience. He wears his glasses.*

The CAPTAIN *starts as if he has just heard something. The* CAPTAIN *stares around the room. Nothing.*

The CAPTAIN *returns to his game. He tries to make his cards come out right. They won't. Exasperated, the* CAPTAIN *gathers his cards, goes over to the French doors and flings them over the battlements outside.*

The CAPTAIN *goes to the wardrobe. The wind blows. The French doors bang and make him jump. The* CAPTAIN *stares around the room then extracts three whiskey bottles hidden at the very back of the wardrobe. The* CAPTAIN *goes to the French doors and throws the bottles over the battlements. The* CAPTAIN *gathers up his boxes of cigars and throws them after the bottles. The* SENTRY *sees everything but does not react.*

The CAPTAIN *takes his glasses off, polishes the lenses with a handkerchief, then tests them to see how well he sees with them. Useless. He throws the spectacles out through the French doors and over the battlements, then stumbles across the room to the desk, on top of which stands a candelabra. By using his fingers to feel what he is doing, he lights the six candles in the candelabra.*

As he blows out the match, the CAPTAIN *notices the laurel wreath on the back of the chair. He picks up the wreath and turns towards the French doors. Then he thinks better of what he is about to do. He cleans the wreath with the cloth draped over the piano then hangs it back on the portrait of* ALICE.

The CAPTAIN *goes to the piano. He punches the keyboard several times. Then he slams the lid shut, locks it and throws the key over the battlements like everything else.*

There is another candelabra with candles on the piano. The CAPTAIN *lights these. Then he goes to the whatnot on which there are several family photographs. He takes a photograph of* ALICE *from its frame, tears up the photograph and scatters the pieces on the floor.*

The French doors blow in the wind and startle the CAPTAIN *again. He calms himself down. There are photographs of his son and his daughter in frames on the whatnot. He takes these photographs out of their frames, kisses them, then slides them inside his tunic near his heart.*

There still remain a couple of framed photographs of ALICE. *He sweeps these as well as the empty frames on to the floor, and then stamps on the lot.*

After all his exertions the CAPTAIN *is tired. He slumps down at the writing table with the telegraph apparatus on it. His heart is hurting. He lights the writing candles and lets out a long drawn out sigh. He now believes there's something moving around the room but he can't make it out. In the end he decides it's a hallucination.*

The CAPTAIN *lumbers back to the desk, lowers the flap and pulls out a bundle of letters tied with a blue ribbon. He hurries to the stove, opens the door, and throws the letters into the flames. He returns to the desk and closes the flap.*

Suddenly, there is a noise, like a creaking floorboard. Very spooky, very startling. The CAPTAIN *looks around anxiously, his hand on his heart. He is looking for something lurking in the shadows. It is there, tantalizingly close, almost within earshot, almost within vision, but he can't see it.*

He gets up and goes across to the door leading to the kitchen and listens with his ear against the wood. Silence. He opens the door suddenly as if he expects to catch someone on the other side but there is no one there.

Suddenly, the telegraph taps once behind him and he jumps: the CAPTAIN *starts at the telegraph apparatus as if he is expecting a message but nothing follows; it was only the time signal. The* CAPTAIN *goes out through the kitchen door and returns after a few moments with the cat.*

The CAPTAIN *sits down and begins to stroke the cat. Silence. The* CAPTAIN *stands up and, with the cat thrown over his shoulder, goes back through the door to the kitchen. Silence, then the sound of someone at the front door.*

ALICE *comes in from the porch. Her hair is pinned up again, the hairpiece*

*is back in place and the grey hair is hidden.. She is elegantly dressed in a walking
coat, hat and gloves. She peers into the room and sees that there is no one
around.*

ALICE *turns and signals out through the front door.* CONOR *suddenly
appears in view and sidles in after her. He looks nervous.*

36) Yes, the riddle and the use of the word of forbearing they don't
work. Could I suggest the text is amended (cut) to read as follows:

CAPTAIN: So then what's the point?
CONOR: There isn't a point ... it's a mess, that's the point ... yet you've
got to get down on your knees in front of it—
CAPTAIN: Bow before the unknown—
CONOR: There is no alternative.
CAPTAIN: If you say ... but how come you're so philosophical, so patient
about everything if it's all just ... chaos?
CONOR: Don't imagine I'm always like this.
CAPTAIN: My guiding principle was always eliminate and move on. No
one suffered on this earth the way I did when I was young ... so before
I joined the army, I stuffed every childhood sorrow and adolescent
defeat into a bag and I drowned the lot in the Irish sea. After that it was
as if the pain had never happened.
CONOR: I know.
CAPTAIN: But what else could I do? I couldn't have gone on otherwise!

37) Yes, let's change it:

CAPTAIN: A wheeler-dealer but a good enough fellow.
CONOR: And the Quarter Master?

38) Yes, let's change it:

CONOR: You spoke of my patience. You have it in buckets yourself.
Where's yours from?

39) Yes let's change it:

ALICE: You won't get this in a bag and bury it at sea.
CAPTAIN: You're an evil schemer, I've never doubted that, but I haven't
a clue what you're saying—
ALICE: If I could undo what I've done ... I'd love you ... I'd take care of
you, Edgar.

40) Yes:

CAPTAIN [*sitting down again*]**:** It's a draw. I stopped you escaping ... you failed to kill me. Oh, and I know that you tried to have me arrested ... but you know, Hibbert and I, we didn't do anything. [ALICE *is astonished.*] But don't worry, that's buried at sea already. [ALICE *is silent.*] Anyway, its not the worst you've done—

41) Yes, what about:

CAPTAIN: Isn't modern life tedious? Once upon a time one fought and fell out, now everyone just quarrels and then makes up straight away. No doubt Conor'll propose the toast at our silver wedding. Haverty will be there, and his awful wife, and Hibbert, *and* McBride ... Colonel Beggs'll gate crash, naturally. Do you remember that wedding in Armagh, when Peter ... Peter Kelly got married to that girl ... she had to wear the ring on the right hand because he'd cut off the finger on her left in that fight they had!

Finally, your last point (not numbered) regarding the transition from *Part One* to *Part Two*. Alice doesn't start *Part Two* hell-bent on radical vengeance. She starts *Part Two* as she ended one, a simmering volcano, ready to explode under the right circumstances but not looking for trouble. That speech in *Part One* where she speaks of herself and Edgar as being welded remains, at the start of *Part Two* an accurate description of the nature of the relationship. They are engaged in a Dance of Death; they have tried to part from each other and the experience has taught them they can't. (Or so they believe. Of course Strindberg's opinion would be that if they wanted too they could part, only they don't because they don't want to. The way Alice and Edgar talk about their relationship is self-serving. They could leave each other if they really wanted to only they can't because they're too much in hate with one another).

What happens in *Part Two*, the story of *Part Two*, is that when Edgar starts to improvise, he sets in motion his own downfall. Edgar's decision to try to marry Judith to the Colonel (probably something of a pipe dream) is something Alice can see the sense off. They don't have money; if Judith can be married to a rich old man, well, why not. And she says as much to Aidan. Her attitude to the youth follows on from this. She knows Aidan is barking up the wrong tree in chasing after Judith because she knows the Captain wants to marry Judith off and, furthermore, Alice knows that she supports the Captain. That's why she takes the hanky back and tells Aidan he's going to study and get off the island. She wants to save Aidan from being hurt by her daughter. (Perhaps, in Aidan, she sees the

Conor she loved as a girl). Towards Johnston, on the other hand, she feels indifference. He's older; he should be able to look after himself.

Alice does not embark on the play with the intention of wreaking havoc, as I said. However, as events unfold in *Part Two*, she realises that perhaps, perhaps, fate has delivered into her hands the means to hurt and harm the Captain—and hating him as she does, she's always on the look out for anything that could provide her with such an opportunity. (Improvisation is a theme of *Part Two* and the way she gets to hurt the man she hates—the way Alice gets to fire her real bullets is completely unexpected, which accounts in some part, for the power of the piece).

It happens like this. Judith makes her damaging telephone call to the Colonel and then runs off with Aidan; this is completely unexpected. Alice had always planned that Judith and the Colonel would make friends, at the very least, just as her husband wanted. However, the telephone call and the elopement, once they have occurred, are seized upon by Alice; here they are, the real bullets she has been waiting all her life to fire.

The killing itself, is a two bullet job. First there's the Colonel's telegram—which not only signals the end of Edgar's hopes for a romantic relationship between the Colonel and his daughter, but also the end of Edgar's relationship with the Colonel. This information wounds the Captain but doesn't finish him off. No, the means of dispatch is Judith's letter which Alice reads aloud and this finishes the Captain off because he realises from its contents that not only has he lost the one he loves and whom he has moulded in his image (Judith) but she has escaped from his thrall and worse, formed an alliance with the son of the man Edgar hates with particular energy, the man who tried to steal his wife, or so he believes. When Edgar hears Judith's letter, what he learns is not only that he's lost a daughter but also, and this is far worse, he learns that he has been completely outmanoeuvred, and encircled, and so great is the shock of defeat, he dies. But none of this is planned, as I keep saying; this isn't Alice's endgame when she starts; her hope at the front of *Part Two* is to survive Edgar and see Judith married (maybe). Then circumstances (entirely of the Captain's making) allow her to fire real bullets and kill her enemy and take the man whom she has always wanted, Conor. But it's all an accident and the woman at the end must know that she is the lucky beneficiary of quite extraordinary luck. Finally, in my opinion this is also Strindberg's line.

Finally, 'The Ride of the Whiteboys'—that's just a title, not an actual piece of music. However, I'm sure there's a malevolent jig or polka out there which will fit the bill.

Tyga goes into hospital Jan. 25th, and I would think that for about ten days thereafter I'll be available for telephonic communication but will find it hard to put pen to paper. Hence I am replying to the list of queries (I got them this morning) as quickly as I have.

Goodness what a long fax.

Warmest wishes

Carlo Gébler

PS: Is it *Dance of Death* or '*The* Dance of Death'? The former, probably.

[1] Store Keeper, according to my OED, would have been the official army term in the nineteenth; however, I think your change would be judicious as Store Keeper sounds too civilian whereas Quarter Master sounds military.

LETTER 14

9th February, 1998

Dear Nick

Your questions.

1) Barmy. What about:

ALICE: He's worse than usual.
CONOR: Shot to hell!
ALICE: He's worse than usual.

I see this exchange as one where Conor overstates (or over-dramatises) and Alice has to correct him (politely); the Captain hasn't lost the plot—or Alice wouldn't want Conor to think this—he's just worse than usual.

2) Boss.

We thought we liked this word instead of chief, didn't we? and the more I think on't, the more I like it. I looked it up in my OED which says that originally it was an American term meaning master and is now widely used in Britain. The dictionary is organised on historical principles and certainly G.B. Shaw was using boss in the sense of master by the mid-thirties. The previous entry is dated 1870 and I can't tell if the writer is English or American but I'm not quite certain that matters. Conor's been in America for ten or twelve years. Couldn't he have picked up boss over there and brought it home with him?

3) Page 27:

CONOR: Come on, what I've seen tonight, this is hell. [*Silence*]

CAPTAIN: You have no idea how I'm torn apart.
CONOR: Literally?
CAPTAIN: Not the body.
CONOR: Oh, these are spiritual torments. There isn't a third kind, is there. [*Pause*]
CAPTAIN [*standing*]: I can't die.

As I read it, Conor's saying well, either you're torn apart physically or psychologically, those are the two kinds of hurt on earth. When the Captain doesn't answer he says, Well, there isn't a third kind, is there? and what he means is, Come on, make your mind up, Edgar, which is it, physiological or spiritual? At this moment I think he's partly irritated and partly wanting to get down to brass tacks and know exactly what it is that's under discussion.

The alternative is to cut the reference to the third type of torment in which case the text would go thus:

CONOR: Come on, what I've seen tonight, this is hell. [*Silence*]
CAPTAIN: You have no idea how I'm torn apart.
CONOR: Literally?
CAPTAIN: Not the body.
CONOR: Oh, these are spiritual torments. [*Pause*]
CAPTAIN [*standing*]: I can't die.

Conor can still play it irritated, can still play it like a man intent on getting down to brass tacks.

I sent a description earlier today on how the play came to be written and I hope it fits the bill.

When we read through *Part Two* next week, which draft will we be using? And what time would you like me at the Tricycle? Or do we meet somewhere else?

A local company here (Tinderbox) want to do a reading of *How to Murder a Man* in April sometime. Is this all right. Naturally I will mention that the play was developed by the Tricycle. I'll also give a short reading from the novel (based on the play) which is being published April 2nd.

My father's funeral wasn't too terrible, all things considered. No, I'll re-phrase that; it was really quite good. We all drove down on Friday morning—the only hitch was that Georgia was violently sick (Ribena and porridge) at Kells which is about half-way to Dublin. We made Glasnevin in good time (to clean up) and admire the coffin that was in the chapel before my father.

Then our hearse turned up with a rather yellow, very piney coffin in the back. I'd asked for the handles to be removed (my father, a no-frills man, would have loathed them—these were brass and very showy) but of course this hadn't been done. Oh well, I thought, you can't have everything. My mother turned up, holding a great bunch of flowers, accompanied by my brother, soon followed by my half-brother (diffident, cripplingly shy—he'd never met any of the family before except for me so this partly accounted for his nervousness), Linda (my half-brother's girlfriend) and Jeananne Crowley (the actress) for whom my dad had lifelong thing. There were also one or two other people I didn't recognise who I later gathered were cousins called Dacks and who I'd never met before.

At one sharp, we trooped into the chapel and took our seats. The chapel was slightly less melancholy than the one in Golders Green but only slightly. In came the ghastly coffin and then came the readings. I did a John Clare poem ('The Faithful and the True'), my brother recited a sonnet, my mother spoke for a few moments and then recited a few lines of Joyce (who my father liked in his envious way); then it was Jeananne Crowley's turn. She read for six minutes from a quasi-love letter my father had written her. Then I went back up to the podium—read a bit of Camus, put on the tape (the adagio section from Shostakovich's 7th Symphony, the 'Leningrad'—it was my father's favourite piece of music) and as the music warbled (I'd made the recording off my Dad's actual record so it was full of cracks and hisses) we watched the coffin trundle through the curtain and into the furnace area beyond. Then it was off to the Shelbourne for a roast beef lunch. Not a bad day at all, really.

Hope you are well, *Dance of Death* is flourishing, etc.

With warmest wishes

Carlo

LETTER 15

Tuesday 17th Febuary, 1998

Dear Nick,

I approached the read-through yesterday quaking with terror. This was line anxiety of course. But within seconds this anxiety disappeared. This had little to do with the qualities of the text and a great deal to do with the way in which the lines were performed—which was brilliantly, strongly, intriguingly, theatrically. I very quickly stopped thinking about the lines (as I listened) because I became *immediately* caught up in the events and characterisation. The cast are wonderful. They're going to be brilliant. You're going to have a great production on your hands which will re-bound to *your* and the *theatre's* credit hugely—no doubt about it. The set's good too. All I would say that matters now (since the cast are obviously only going to get better in the weeks ahead—accent-wise, performance-wise, every-wise) is that what everyone needs to have in their minds is the story. The narrative is a very complicated, dense, Swiss watch mechanism to which everyone contributes hugely. So everyone must know what bit of the story they're carrying. But as everyone watches the whole thing in the weeks to come, everyone will become inscribed with an internal sense of the narrative trajectory and that can only make the production stronger.

Now some thoughts which I had after the finish and I was on my way back to Enniskillen. (Isn't that always the way?) and all concerning Tim Woodward—Conor.

Point one. Conor, in a sense, is us. He represents the audience within the madhouse that is Alice and Edgar's home. He has, so to speak, one foot on the stage and the other on our side of the footlights in the front stalls. I'm not saying, by the way, that he should be in eye contact with the audience or play to us in a 'Brechtian way'; what I am saying is that he is, like us, an observer who sees their lunacy (which Alice and Edgar don't). And that's why what one can speak of as his charm, or his Dave Allen type presentation style, or what ever it is, is so important. As he smiles in the midst of insanity, as he makes his perfectly reasonable observations, or asks his perfectly reasonable questions and tries to understand what is going on, the audience will be with him going, Yes, absolutely, you're absolutely right, you ask him, you ask her. If he immediately becomes like Edgar and Alice and withdraws his foot from the stalls so to speak, and stops being our representative in the House of Misery, something will be lost. The trick therefore, for Tim, will be to demonstrate how the sane one (himself) gradually gets embroiled in Edgar and Alice's life in the course of *Part One*, and how he struggles to escape and fails in *Part Two*.

Point two—I'm still on the charm front—I read an interesting anecdote about Strindberg in Meyer's biog of Strindberg. (It's wonderful by the way, the biog.) which I thought was very Conor. One evening, in the Black Porker pub in Berlin, a beautiful woman swept in and demanded a kiss from August Strindberg. Our author was sat drinking in his corner. Without batting an eyelid he stood, removed his coat, made his way to the woman and began to kiss her passionately and lengthily—so lengthily in fact, that a friend took out his watch and was heard to observe "Over two minutes." Strindberg then broke off his embrace with this nineteenth century equivalent of the Kissagram, returned to his table, put his coat back on again, and sat down.[1] The woman who demanded the kiss presumably did not expect the great misogynist to oblige (and therefore intended to embarrass our August) but Strindberg, with his surprising response, turned the tables. And yet how he did it seems to me so very Conor. There was no bluster or agression or unpleasantness. On the contrary, Strindberg's manner of dealing with the strange woman was charming and amusing and deft and that's Conor to a T. He's always charming and amusing and quick (except on the rare occasions when he loses the plot); Conor always does the right thing. What he can't cope with is a) the Capt. getting hold of his son (although he becomes reconciled to this in *Part Two*) and b) Alice getting under his skin (he never gets reconciled to this).

Point three—Tim asked me whether Conor means it when he says men make promises fully believing they will keep these promises. (He's talking to Alice about what men say when they marry). Yesterday I said I didn't think Conor meant what he said; however, on reflection I've changed my mind. Why shouldn't this be an occasion when Conor means what he says and says what he means. After all, the capacity to tell the truth, to tell it like it is, is a very important aspect of charm.

And that's it; this is only a short letter. (No long letters for you—you're far too busy). I'm available for telephone communication at all hours of day and night. My fax isn't working (although I can send faxes from my computer) and once again—well done, brilliant, fabulous, it's great—and I'm not just saying it—*it really is going to be great.*

Warmest from here (where spring has started and the snowdrops are out)

Carlo Gébler

[1] See *Strindberg: A Biography*, Meyer, London 1985 pge. 257/8

LETTER 16

Wednesday 25th March, 1998

Dear Nick,

I've been reading (or re-reading I should say) *Part Two* since we spoke an hour or so ago. I have also re-read Strindberg's end and compared the two versions. This is one of the parts of the play (of *Part Two* I mean) that's probably closest to the original (with the exception of the very last line from Alice). I think the reason for this fidelity (on my part) was that as I was writing I imagined Strindberg's end was the anchor in the wall of the tightrope across which I was going to stagger. Does this make sense? I wanted to keep it the way it was because that was I felt safe.

Now we've spoken several times about the end and it's not working and we've tried several ways with what we've got and it's still not working. Hummh. It's especially not working, if I understand you rightly, from the point of view of Tim, who is playing Conor, and who has to go through a number of mood changes which seem to him (I hope I've got this right too) somewhat improbable.

In a situation like this I often find that the best thing is to go back to first principles. What is Conor? First of all he's a man of strong, overwhelming, uncontrollable urges. These are unknown to him very often, until they seize him. Why does he go to the island? For Alice of course. It is also true if we had him on the Freudian couch as the events of the plays are unfolding, that he would deny this, or he would certainly not be aware of it.

As far as he understands himself, Conor has gone to the island for all those bland, obvious reasons. He wants to go back to Ireland and rehabilitate himself; Dublin is too public a place to start (given his divorce, a *very* rare thing in those days) but Crookedstone, as an out of the way place, is the perfect location for such a project. He wants to be near Derry where his son is a cadet. He wants to be near Alice (in a platonic way, he thinks) and re-connect with his youth. His is the form of middle-age that takes an overly indulgent view of returning to roots and family and the known. Then there is the Donegal constituency. He might know (and I think he does) that there's a possible opening coming up. On Crookedstone he's ideally placed to contest the constituency. If he were in Wexford, of course, it would be out of the question. He also wants to be busy. He's one of those people who doesn't like to be idle. Conor is a man who likes to be always doing. He likes to be of service. He likes to be of help. Look how he helps the Dawson's in myriad ways all the way through the narrative. But, as I said, his real reason, which is Alice, that he doesn't know or recognise; that's buried, well sublimated.

And then, through the most extraordinary (and unpredicted) turn of events, the Captain dies. Furthermore, irony of ironies, the Captain's death is precipitated by his, the Captain's own actions. If the Captain hadn't set the Colonel hare running, if he hadn't plotted, and meddled and been his usual busy body self, if he hadn't built the house of Cards that he builds in *Part Two*, then the calamities which overcome him at the end of *Part Two* would not have overcome him and he would have lived. But the Captain's nature is to meddle and interfere and, in so doing, he unleashes the demons that destroy him.

Alice's position *vis-a-vis* all this is pretty straightforward. The marriage is a bad one and, frankly, she is not unperturbed by the turn in events. Of course after the death, and in some measure prompted by Johnson's presence which reminds her that the garrison is full of gossiping tongues, she reins in her true feelings and decides it would not be prudent to let them show. It is also the case, as you said on the phone, that once Edgar is dead he is dead. The fact that there is a huge space at the end where Edgar once was is an enormous fact which Alice *immediately seizes*. With Edgar dead life is different for her instantly and she realises, very quickly, that she doesn't need to keep the vendetta up for any longer. She realises she can be generous and she realises, most importantly of all, that life has delivered this enormous gift, Conor (and as always, life delivers Conor in the most unexpected way).

For Alice the end is a revelation—it's about the only one she has. But for Conor it is simply the nth of a long line of revelations that have been striking him from the moment he walked on stage in *Part One*. Conor is the opposite of Edgar; he can grasp a plot or a scheme, yes, but he's not by nature a plotter or a schemer; he's not one of life's chess players. Things happen and he's amazed or surprised or puzzled. He's also (which is another part of his non-chess playing personality) someone who doesn't ever like to be thought ill of. On the contrary, he likes to be liked (that's why he makes himself so endlessly useful) and he definitely doesn't like to fall out. Only when he's really pushed (as he is over the business with his son at the end of *Part One*) is he prepared to contemplate taking decisive action, and then only temporarily. He backs down, of course. It isn't that he hasn't the bottle. It's that he believes that justice really does win out in the end. He also believes that malevolence, if you give in to it, gives you cancer. Finally, he's a man who, while he won't countenance illegality (Edgar's embezzlement) is really not up for the Captain's humiliation. He's not that type.

So what is happening at the end of *Part Two?* Well, up to the bottom of the penultimate page—'Well, there'll be fine words at his funeral alright,' I presume everything is ticking over nicely and we have no problems. Edgar is dead and Johnston has brought the news. And the Captain's last words. So what is going through Conor's mind now? The talk about the wreaths at top of the last page is clear (I hope). The death will be public. Everyone will be there. The subtext is that Alice and Conor will have to be on their guard. Then Alice drops her bombshell. She doesn't want to speak ill of Edgar. Except it's not really a bombshell is it? Johnston is still there. She can mean it but we can take it she also wants Johnston to hear this. Then Johnston goes and we get the first Conor problem:

CONOR: 'They know not what they do.' When I asked you in the past you always said he didn't know what he was doing. He saw opportunites. He took them. If that's right, then you must forgive him.

Could I suggest that we change this speech in two tiny ways so that it reads like this.

CONOR: 'They know not what they do.' When I asked you in the past you always said he didn't know what he was doing *either*. He saw opportunites. He took them. If that's right, then *we* must forgive him.[1]

What I'm suggesting I hope, with these changes, is that what Conor is trying to suggest is that the Captain is as guilty as the rest of humanity (and therefore shouldn't throw stones in glasshouses). It isn't that Alice and Conor are mere mortals to the Captain's Jesus Christ. It's that the Captain is a mere mortal as well. They are three of them on the same level as the thieves on the cross. This can be played as a revelation, Oh my God, I just realised, it's not the Captain's different from us, we're all the bloody same.

Alice replies with a speech that appears to be delivered from another planet ("At last there is peace here," etc.). This is just Alice making the most dramatic capital she can out of the situation. She's also enjoying a moment of quiet triumph. And she's also preparing to play the part of the widow for which she's been studying all her life. (" ... my husband, love of my youth ... ")

Conor replies with, "He was brave and not afraid ... to fight for himself." This starts off as a compliment but ends up as, well, a plain statement. Conor is definitely not a performer like Alice.

Now we get to the really difficult bit. Alice, now returned to earth, responds with her plain truth; "He went through every misery," etc. and it is at this point that I would like to suggest a new line for Conor. At the moment he makes an irritated statement which seem cussed and churlish ("Except he didn't live ... he didn't know how.") It has a touch of the rebuke about it. So what about if he says instead, in a much much more dreamy, uncertain way, as if it has just occured to him (another Conor revelation), *"Except, did he know how to live ... did he know how?"* The subtext is that Edgar didn't know how to be happy but it is only, at this moment with this thought bubbling up into Conor's mind that he, Conor, really realises, really really realises how miserable the Captain was. (Granted, he's talked about the Captain's misery in *Part One*, but this is the moment, now the Captain is dead and no longer exerting his magnetic spell that Conor experiences the true weight of what his friend and enemy went through. This is only possible because the Captain is dead).

Alice is still in reminiscence mode (and practising for playing the garrison widow) and delivers the penultimate line that ends, "I must have loved that man."

Conor responds, "And hated him." Now this is a very difficult line—

especially if Conor's been in churlish, rebuking, cussed mode in his previous line. However, if he's in a dreamy swimming up from the bottom of the sea with a pearl of wisdom mode, then it's just another revelation. "And hated him." Yes, she loved him, she hated him, the man was miserable, it was all a horrible, unspeakable, ghastly dance of death, the whole last twenty-five miserable years. It's not a vengeful statement but a factual statement; it's simply part of the whole revelatory package.

Alice agrees but it's past, it's gone, it's water under the bridge (like Edgar she has a phenomenal capacity for casting away unwanted baggage and recovering psychologically) and she's not going to hold on to the hate any more and now she wants to wish the dead man well. Also, it is also bloody convenient that Edgar's gone, because she and Conor can now pick up the reins where they left off more than a quarter century earlier. They embrace and, frozen in peace, we end.

This is very long. Please ring me if it's not clear. I hope it's of some use. I'm sorry about the dress rehearsal hold up tomorrow but when we made our plans three weeks ago it was a three o'clock start and when I booked the tickets I didn't think to enquire if there'd been any changes in the start. I'll get the express to Paddington and hope to get to you as soon as I can. If I'm delayed I'll ring the theatre to let you know.

BEST AND WARMEST WISHES

Carlo Gébler

[1] I've italicised the two new words.

OTHER DRAMA TITLES

from

LAGAN PRESS

Joseph Tomelty
All Souls' Night & Other Plays
edited and introduced by Damian Smyth

ISBN: 1 873687 04 4
216 pp, £4.95 pbk

Best know as a stage and film actor and as the creator of *The McCooeys*—Northern Ireland's 1940s radio soap which made him a household name in his native place—Joseph Tomelty was also a novelist, short-story writer and, above all, a playwright.

This book, selected by the critic Damian Smyth, gathers for the first time into one volume four major Tomelty plays—the sombre and deeply sad *All Souls' Night* (1948), the lyric *The Singing Bird* (1948), the serio-comic *April in Assagh* (1953) and the controversial *The End House* (1944).

All Souls' Night, set in a dark, passionless world on the east coast of Ulster, is his most critically-acclaimed play. Dealing with poverty, meanness of soul and a mother's consuming greed, it has been described as the best play written in the north of Ireland. It is counterpointed by *April in Assagh*, a play set in a fantastical townland, which is funny and satirical with a dark core of foreboding and published here for the first time. *The End House* creates a Belfast of urban violence after the model of O'Casey. *The Singing Bird*, written for radio in 1948 and later adapted for television, starring Tomelty himself, is a beautiful, pastoral tale of 'a gentle madness'.

Together, these plays provide an indispensable insight into the workings of the double-sided imagination of Tomelty's place— one the one hand deeply obsessive and corrosive, on the other witty, meditative and happy and all with an exhilarating muscular lyricism.

Jennifer Johnston
Three Monologues
Twinkletoes • *Mustn't Forget High Noon* • *Christine*
ISBN: 1 873687 70 2
72 pp, £4.95 pbk

Collected for the first time in print, these monologues represent one of the many dimensions of the talent of Jennifer Johnston, one of Ireland's most important writers since the war.

Revolving round the griefs and traumas caused by the troubles in the north of Ireland, they are an exploration of individual survivals in the midst of the disintegration of life and lives.

Twinkletoes is the story of Karen, a top IRA prisoner's wife; looked up to by her community, she cannot express her loneliness. *Mustn't Forget High Noon* introduces Billy Maltseed, a border Protestant, who has just lost his best friend, a UDR part-timer, shot by the IRA. In *Christine*, Billy's southern Irish wife mourns his death by violence which leaves her alone and childless in a community riven by suspicion.

These monologues—by turns comic and intensely moving—together reclaim the individual voice in the teeth of stereotypes, expressing most vividly the human beneath the inhuman and the headlines.

Martin Lynch
Three Plays
Dockers • *The Interrogation of Ambrose Fogarty* • *Pictures of Tomorrow*
edited and introduced by Damian Smyth
ISBN: 1 873687 60 5
224 pp, £4.95 pbk

Martin Lynch has been a significant figure in Irish drama since the late 1970s when *They are Taking Down the Barricades* gave expression to contemporary Belfast working-class life. Rooted among the political and imaginative forces bearing upon and emerging from both northern communities, Lynch explored those forces with humour, anger and compassion.

Having committed himself to the values of community-based drama, he wrote a string of popular successes throughout the 1980s. Marked by an accurate ear for dialogue and a pungent wit, the plays chalked out a territory securely his own. Out of this commitment have come also three of the most important plays in the last twenty-five years from the north of Ireland—*Dockers, The Interrogation of Ambrose Fogarty* and *Pictures of Tomorrow.*

Dockers is a boisterous recreation of working-class life in Belfast's famed Sailortown district. Reminiscent of Dario Fo but rigorously rooted in the sadness of real political conflict, *The Interrogation of Ambrose Fogarty* is a most vivid, pointed and funny play dealing with the ironies and absurdities of police detention. With *Pictures of Tomorrow*, Lynch attempts to deal with the disillusion of left-wing ideals in the wake of the collapse of communism, against the poignant backdrop of the Spanish Civil War, a conflict loaded with Irish resonances.

These plays, available for the first time, establish Martin Lynch as a leading Irish playwright of his generation.

Jennifer Johnston
The Desert Lullaby
ISBN: 1 873687 26 5
56 pp, £4.95 pbk

One of Ireland's most import post-war prose writers, Jennifer Johnston has established a reputation as a playwright of rare moral and imaginative force. Her dramatic narratives, *Twinkletoes, Mustn't Forget High Noon* and *Christine*—collected by Lagan Press under the title *Three Monologues*—were produced to critical and popular acclaim by the Abbey Theatre, Dublin.

Moving between the Ireland of the 'Emergency' and the present day, *The Desert Lullaby* is the story of two old women: the 'harmless insane' Flora and Nellie, her housekeeper, scold and protector. Their intertwining stories provide an evocative exploration of familial love, oppression, loyalty and memory. Rooted firmly in the imaginative and political tensions at the heart of Ireland past and present, their voices, stories and perspectives—young and old—are an articulation of endurance in the face of greater impersonal forces of destruction: loss, death, decay and betrayal.

By turns comic and harrowing, *The Desert Lullaby* confirms Jennifer Johnston as one of Ireland's most significant dramatists.

Jennifer Johnston's prose works include *The Captain's and the Kings* (1972), *How Many Miles to Babylon* (1974), *Shadows on Our Skin* (1977), *The Christmas Tree* (1981), *The Railway Station Man* (1984), *Fool's Sanctuary* (1987) and *The Invisible Worm* (1991). Her most recent novel is *The Illusionist* (1995).

Sam Thompson
Over the Bridge & Other Plays
edited and introduced by John Keyes
ISBN: 1 873687 66 4
256 pp, £5.95 pbk

"During the Westminster election of 1964, when Lord O'Neill of the Maine was still plain Captain at the Northern Irish helm, he made reference to 'a certain Mr. Sam Thompson whose past experience is, I gather, in producing works of fiction'. A lot of blood has since flowed under the bridge: it is a sarcasm to which posterity has not been kind. Bridges are a favourite Ulster metaphor. 'Bridge building between the communities' has become the compulsory sport of our captains and our kings. The traditional sport of stirring up sectarian hatreds, however, continues to be played at times of stress, like election campaigns, or when deciding upon a suitably provocative name for an actual steel and concrete bridge. Going over the Bridge is another activity entirely, demanding a degree of guts and an integrity which public life in Ireland has failed to cultivate, to say the least. Sam Thompson dedicated his life to it. He coaxed, commanded, persuaded and implored his mulish fellow-countrymen to make the journey. He wasn't a captain or a king but a shipyard painter and they listened to him. They knew the reality of his fiction ... "—Stewart Parker

Pivotal in the development of modern Irish drama, Sam Thompson marks the début of an authentic urban voice on stage. *Over the Bridge* (1960), produced in the face of hostility from the unionist establishment, is an indictment of sectarianism in people's working lives. His second play, *The Evangelist* (1963), directed by Hilton Edwards to critical acclaim, explores the fanaticism and hypocrisy deforming religion while his last play, *Cemented with Love* (1965) exposes the corruption of political life in the north of Ireland.

Complete with an introduction by critic and theatre historian John Keyes, *Over the Bridge & Other Plays* is a compelling imaginative investigation of the tensions underpinning northern Irish life.

Owen McCafferty
Mojo Mickybo
ISBN: 1 873687 53 2
56 pp, £5.95 pbk

Mojo Mickybo, the latest play from the Belfast playwright Owen McCafferty, is an exploration of the imaginative liberations of childhood against a background of dehumanising poverty and deep-rooted communal hatred.

A tale of two boys in the early 1970s—one from up the road and the other from over the bridge—whose brief friendship centres round playing headers, torturing old Rip the Balls, building huts, spitting from cinema balconies and *Butch Cassidy and the Sundance Kid*, the plays portrays unsentimentally, yet with affection, true innocence and protests eloquently at its betrayal.

Vibrant and fast-paced, *Mojo Mickybo* sings with a streetwise lyricism and an acute social and political insight into the faultlines which underlie the north of Ireland. Yet, above all else, McCafferty writes with veracity yet with a compassionate eye for the failings and flaws of his characters as they struggle against circumstances and, indeed, themselves.

Owen McCafferty has written many plays for the stage including *Winners, Losers & Non-Runners* (1992), *I Won't Dance Don't Ask Me* (1993), *The Private Picture Show* (1994), *The Waiting List* (1994), *Freefalling* (1996) and *Shoot the Crow* (1997). His *Plays & Monologues* was recently published by Lagan Press.

£1.99.